Belinda Hadden has written publications on travel, fas... *Tatler*, *Over 21*, the *Evening Standard*, and the *Daily Mail*. She is also the author of *The Ageing Parent Handbook* and *The Over 60's Directory*, and has exhibited at the Royal Academy Summer Exhibition. She is married with three children and nearly lives in Chelsea.

Amanda Christie has inherited the dry wit of her father Derek Nimmo and has written or participated in features for the *Daily Mail*, *Harpers & Queen* and many other publications. She has also toured extensively as both an actress and stage manager. Amanda is married to film director Willie Christie, has three children and lives in Chelsea.

Sweet Revenge

—∞—

200 delicious ways to get your own back

Belinda Hadden and
Amanda Christie

With cartoons by Ian Jackson

HEADLINE

First published in 1995
by HEADLINE BOOK PUBLISHING

10 9 8 7 6 5 4 3

ISBN 0 7472 5338 2

Typeset by
Letterpart Limited, Reigate, Surrey

Printed and bound in Great Britain by
Cox & Wyman Ltd, Reading, Berks

HEADLINE BOOK PUBLISHING
A division of Hodder Headline PLC
338 Euston Road
London NW1 3BH

For our ultimate revenge this book is dedicated to the following people who have wronged us in one way or another: SS, AR, RB, MW, AH, GC, WL, KH, DM, EA, LH, F, PW, DB and MW . . . you know who you are!

However, we *would* like to thank:
Josie Ashcroft, Vicky Barnsley, Charlie Barton, Sid and Susie Beart, Johnny Bevan, David Briggs, Alan Brooke, John Brown, Duncan Bullivant, Alister Campbell, Sue Carroll, Fiona Corkhill, Dudley Davenport, Nigel Dempster, Adam Edwards, Margie Fenwick, Medina Gilbey, Tom Goldstaub, Corinna Gordon, Nicky Gray, Julian Grazebrook, Christopher Hanbury, Iain Harris-Bartlett, Adam Helliker, Stuart Higgins, Aziz Laghzaoui, Dai Llewellyn, Jonathan Lloyd, Paul Matcham, Eva McGaw, Iain McGowan, Michael Naylor-Leyland, Julia Samuel, Urs Schwarzenbach, Mike Smith and Sarah Greene, Taki Theodoracopulos, Diane Wilson, Les Wilson, Victoria Wooderson, and, last but by no means least, Abel Hadden and Willie Christie.

Contents

— ∞ —

	Foreword by Derek Nimmo	1
1.	Love and Disharmony	5
2.	Sexual Subterfuge	23
3.	Nasty Neighbours	43
4.	Road Hogs	51
5.	Office Politics	63
6.	Little Angels	77
7.	An Englishman's Home . . .	83
8.	Looking Good?	93
9.	Cash Crises	107
10.	Military Mischief	117
11.	Animal Antics	131
12.	Telephone Trouble	151
13.	Culinary Capers	159
14.	Photographic Evidence	175
15.	Travellers' Tales	179
16.	Acting Up	191
17.	Quick Tricks and Devilish Deeds	201

Foreword

— ∞ —

I am writing this on one of the hottest days of the English summer of '95. Outside the window a cloudless sky. The shady trees in my garden beckon invitingly. The goldfish are rising in the way the salmon didn't on the Blackwater in June. Why am I indoors? Well, quite simply because I received a fax from my vengeful daughter this morning commanding me to write a foreword to this rather dubious collection of anecdotes gathered together by Amanda and her companion-in-charms, Belinda Hadden.

Amanda and Belinda have been close friends since schooldays. They have a keen sense of the ridiculous and complementary senses of humour. The highlight of their week used to be parading the Kings Road on a Saturday afternoon in a variety of fancy dress costumes. Yashmaks were great favourites but dressing up as the lead singers from ABBA came a close second.

Earlier this year they did a feature on wine buying in France for Auto Express Magazine (under the mistaken impression that it was for The *Sunday* Express) and it was only a matter of time before they embarked upon a major opus together. The idea for *Sweet Revenge* was born. Since then they have written to everyone they know and hundreds of people they don't. My address book has been pillaged – perhaps that is why the book has a fair share of theatrical stories – here are two more, both concerning the writer/director/actor Orson Welles.

1

One Saturday during the production of his film *The Lady From Shanghai*, Welles decided that a certain set needed repainting for the following Monday's filming. Having been told by the Production Manager, Jack Fier, that this was quite impossible, Welles gathered together a group of friends. They broke into the Paint Department late on Saturday evening, repainted the set themselves, and left a huge sign over the entrance to the studio 'THE ONLY THING WE HAVE TO FEAR IS FIER HIMSELF'. When the official set painters arrived for work on Monday, they immediately called a strike. Fier was obliged to pay a hefty sum to each member of the crew as compensation for the work done by non-Union labour. He obtained his revenge by deducting the money from Welles's fee and had a new banner painted 'ALL'S WELL THAT ENDS WELLES'.

Upon another occasion, the Film Director, Vincent Korda and his son, Michael, had to chase Orson Welles, who was running from contract obligations, across Europe. Landing in Venice and pursuing him through Naples, Capri and Nice, they finally caught up with him in Cagnes-sur-Mer and hoisted him off to a private aeroplane. Michael Korda and Orson shared the back seats with a giant basket of fruit, which Vincent had carefully selected in Nice, wedged between them. Michael eventually fell asleep. When he awoke, he eyed the basket and realised that Welles had systematically taken a single bite out of each piece of fruit. Having thus effectively destroyed Vincent's fruit, Welles now slept soundly. His immaculate appearance was marred only by a few spots of juice on his shirt front.

Perhaps one of the most spectacular acts of revenge was perpetrated in the early 19th Century by the playwright and composer Theodore Edward Hook. It appears that he had a score to settle with a Mrs Tottenham, who lived at 34 Berner Street in London. Records do not relate what had occasioned his anger. What Hook did was to write an enormous number of letters – more than 4,000 of them. As a result of these, on a particular day there arrived at 34 Berner Street an armada of vehicles, some delivering coal, some furniture, one other a wedding cake. There were hearses and haycarts; there were chimney-sweeps, butchers, bakers, candlestick makers, lawyers, doctors, dentists, fishmongers and every other conceivable kind of tradesman. The confusion was completed by the arrival of the Duke of Gloucester, The Lord Mayor of London and a host of other dignitaries, lured to Berner Street on some pretext or other in one of Hook's letters. Hook, who had rented a room on the opposite side of the street, was able to sit by the window and enjoy the spectacle.

Probably the most effective revenge anyone can attain is in their last Will and Testament – as my daughter will one day find out. For damning dismissals, however, few Wills can match that of a successful industrialist who died in Philadelphia in 1947 leaving the following:–

'To my wife I leave her lover and the knowledge that I wasn't the fool she thought I was.

To my son I leave the pleasure of earning a living. For twenty-five years he thought the pleasure was mine. He was mistaken.

To my daugher I leave $100,000. She will need it. The only piece of business her husband ever did was to marry her.

To my Valet I leave the clothes he has been stealing from me for ten years. Also the fur coat he wore last summer when I was in Palm Beach.

To my Chauffeur I leave my cars. He almost ruined them and I want him to have the satisfaction of finishing the job.

To my Partner I leave the suggestion that he take some clever man in with him at once if he expects to do any business.'

I am now going back to my deck chair. To forget wrong is the best revenge.

Derek Nimmo
August 1995

Love and Disharmony

— ∞ —

'If you want to get revenge on a man, marry him!'
Basia Briggs, 1995

Love and Disharmony

Lord Gillford cannot reveal the identity of the young couple who announced their engagement. Sadly, the groom-to-be discovered, quite by accident, that his fiancée was having an affair with the best man. The groom decided to say nothing and he acted quite normally throughout all the preparations until the wedding day.

The service went off without a hitch and the reception was a delight. At last, it was time for the speeches. The groom stood up and gave a marvellous speech, and made all the traditional thank yous for the flowers, the organist, the bridesmaids . . . and finally, in front of all the guests, he thanked his best man 'who has been screwing my wife for the last few weeks'. While guests stood watching in stunned horror, he scrumpled his speech notes and walked off. The marriage was never consummated so was, therefore, null and void, yet he had the satisfaction of knowing that it cost the bride's family at least £15,000.

∞

Sign seen on a newsagent's bulletin board:
    For Sale: set of Golf Clubs, reasonable condition, £90 o.n.o.
    If a male voice answers the telephone, please hang up!

∞

A sexy love letter found in her boyfriend's pocket prompted a young lady to empty his Chanel aftershave and replace it with kettle descaling fluid. For good measure she also poured oven cleaner into his handmade shoes and covered his suits and silk underwear in black coffee.

∞

It was the same thing every night – Mrs Filsbois would watch with resignation while her husband flirted outrageously with every female under the age of sixty-five. Everybody in every bar and nightclub in the pretty Alpine resort of Zermatt knew the score.

One evening she had had enough and snuck home early. Knowing he would arrive back later, very tired and very drunk, she calmly crushed a bag of crisps into his side of the bed, climbed into her side, and went to sleep. He had the most uncomfortable night of his life.

∞

He told his wife that he was going on a business trip for a long weekend and, instead, he took his lovely mistress to a stunning hotel. He told her he would leave his wife for her and they shared a glorious weekend, at the end of which he unceremoniously dumped her. All she had to remember it by was some hotel soap, a few sheets of the hotel letterhead and a broken heart.

A few days later she posted some lacy underwear and an empty contraceptive packet to her ex-lover's wife, with a letter typed on the hotel's writing paper which read: 'Dear Madam, Following your stay here we found the enclosed items in your bedroom and we return them herewith.'
– Tatler *magazine's social editor, the glamorous Ewa Lewis, was far too discreet to reveal the identity of the well-heeled lady who wrought this revenge.*

∞

Jilted father of two, Mike Owen, took bitter revenge on his cheating wife. He nailed a giant sign painted with the words 'Adulterous Wife' above the 'For Sale' board outside the house he shared with his pretty wife Jane after she had an affair with Ian, the builder who was working on their extension. He also amended his outgoing answerphone message to say, 'Sorry. I cannot speak to you right now. I have got my hands around my adulterous wife's throat. If you would like to leave your name and number after the tone I will return your call as soon as she stops breathing.'

∞

Some years ago in New York a woman hit the headlines when she shot her lover because he had announced he was going to marry someone else. The shot did not kill him and he was rushed to hospital. The revenge shooting completely backfired because, when they were removing the bullet, the doctors discovered a tumour in him and were able to operate successfully to remove it. Thus by shooting him, she actually saved his life which was the last thing she had wanted.

∞

Kathy Lette, author of the splendidly funny Foetal Attraction *and* The Llama Parlour *wrought a revenge which was so sweet and oh, so simple that it has achieved Urban Myth Status. The story is mentioned in her book* Girls Night Out *and here Kathy describes the events in full*:

Looking back I blame it on the man shortage. In Sydney all the men are either married or gay. Or married *and* gay. And the rest have a three grunt vocabulary of 'na', 'dunno' and 'errgh'. Apart from the occasional Pommy

10

poet passing through town, there is nobody. Nothing. Zilch.

That's how I ended up having a close encounter of the grope kind with a MMM (Middle-aged Married Man). Like most of these scenarios, I didn't know he was married until I found the teething ring in his pocket. But by then it was too late. He was tall, dark and bankable with biteable buttocks and . . . I fell in love. (I was young enough not to know that when a man says his wife 'doesn't understand him' what it means is that he wants you under, not standing.)

There were drawbacks. He was forever pulling away from my passionate love bite with a panic-stricken cry of 'Don't mark me!' After a night of heart-felt declarations of adoration and devotion, the next morning I'd pass him in the Woolworth's frozen food aisle . . . and he'd stare straight ahead as if he'd never laid eyes on me.

Even worse was never knowing when he was going to drop around. Invariably it would be the night I was in my pyjammies covered in acne lotion, with one eyebrow plucked, my hair plastered in henna and wearing an organic face mask. A knock at the door would send me torpedoing down to the bathroom. Not wanting to waste my precious R-rated moments with him, I'd hack and scrape away at my legs with a blunt razor in the shower, simultaneously inserting my diaphragm and spraying the old bod with aphrodisiacal unguents. Slashed, trailing blood and covered in Band-Aids, I'd stagger breathlessly up the stairs and into his arms. (It was all right. He just loved my 'girlish charms'.)

He promised he'd leave her. He promised we'd live together with a His and Her Harbour View. Marriage was in the air . . . well, I *thought* it was marriage. What it turned out to be was the car exhaust of his Alfa Romeo as he sped off into the sunset. I truly believed my MMM loved me, but it seemed I was merely a distraction – a little something to break the monogamy.

You can imagine how I felt when he left his wife a few weeks later for a woman *even younger than moi* (a case of upward nubility) and ensconced her in a penthouse apartment with a *His and Her Harbour View*.

There was only one thing to do. My girlfriend distracted the Super while I snatched the key. Once inside I took down the bedroom curtain rail. Removing the stoppers at the ends of the rail I stuffed the hollow cylinder full of prawns, replaced the stoppers and rehung the curtains. Now all I had to do was wait . . .

It was a heat-wave summer. From my girlfriend's flat on the less salubrious side of the street we watched through binoculars as the love-birds tore apart the flat looking for the source of the odour. Within a week, he'd called the 'Rent a Kill' flick man. This was followed by a new carpet. Then, a complete re-wallpapering. We watched them have their first fight. The new girlfriend started sleeping in another room. Then she refused to go back into the apartment. Next, she moved out altogether. Shortly after, the apartment went up for sale.

Revenge is sweet. Sweeter than tiramisu. And, with a broken heart and a wounded ego like mine it was, let's face it, cheaper than therapy.

We watched the removal men pack the van. And the real beauty of it is, *they packed the bedroom curtain rail.*

∞

Lady Sarah Graham-Moon hit the headlines when she took revenge on her cheating husband, Sir Peter Graham-Moon, in spectacular style. Incensed that he had moved in with another woman before their divorce had gone through, she chopped the left arms off thirty-two of his Savile Row suits, tipped six litres of white paint over his beloved BMW and delivered seventy bottles of his vintage wines to neighbouring doorsteps in the Berkshire villages of Lambourne and East Garston where her husband was staying with his new girlfriend. She said: 'I've done my bit and I've run out of things to do now. I'm not loopy – I'm just tired of being used,' advocating that the form of revenge should be tailored to its victim.

There are many people who believe that revenge takes care of itself and you don't need to lift a finger to help it. They are absolutely right in this case. Lady Sarah had the satisfaction of seeing Sir Peter sold down the river by the blonde who replaced her. Terry Graham-Moon revealed her bedroom secrets to the *News of The World* in July this year following her departure from the marital home, with the words: 'He's just a sex-mad dirty old man. Sex with him was so horrible I used to lie back and cry my eyes out until he'd finished – and that could take hours.'

– with thanks to Nigel Dempster, who first revealed the story in the Mail *Diary.*

∞

The two-timing boyfriend had no sense of smell so Shirley, his cheated-upon girlfriend, devised the perfect revenge. She decided to spike his aftershave with pee from a hospital sample. 'It absolutely stank,' said nurse Shirley. It worked. Her rival, having a reasonable sense of smell, became totally disenchanted. He and Shirley are now back together.

∞

Having had a few days to compose herself after she had been dumped by her boyfriend, one young lady decided to weave a little fairytale around the whole episode in order not to lose face. She pretended to all their friends that he was leaving the country to take up a new job in the Far East. To play out her fantasy to the full she

cancelled his milk, his papers and his cleaner and had the electricity, gas and telephone supply terminated. That was before she put his house on the market and sold his car.

∞

'This story relates to a period of much loneliness and intense introspection, after I had come down from Oxford University. A lady whom I had loved, but who had finally grown weary of my pursuit, sent me a postcard depicting the execution block in the Tower of London. On the back she had tersely conveyed the message that I was being given the chop, and that she would be marrying another gentleman – signing it curtly with her initials. The card was dated April 1st 1965.

It so happened that I had in my desk a postcard depicting the Pets' Cemetery at Longleat, which I sent to her by return of post – dating it April 2nd 1965. On the back I inscribed the letters "R.I.P. – A".
– *with thanks to the Marquess of Bath, Alexander Thynne, who adds that, after an interval, they became the best of friends.*

∞

'I heard this story of revenge when I lived in Africa: Daisy and Dick had been married for some time. He was not without his faults but she was the sort of wife that always tried to belittle him in public, especially when it came to his party tricks.

'Dick had learned to read minds. It started as a party trick but often he had a run of luck and was able to say accurately which guest had chosen which object from the array placed on the dining table. Daisy hated the adoration this apparent sixth sense brought to Dick and she was always undermining his glory with the odd remark that "Uri Geller he was *not*." Dick bore this stoically but

16

felt he could have had a little more support from his wife.

'It was when Daisy returned to Johannesburg from Kenya on one of her visits to see her parents who had settled there that Dick knew she had been unfaithful. One of the many habits that Dick had that irritated Daisy was his smoking. He had tried many times to give up the habit but the will was always too weak – another Achilles' heel for Daisy to stick a barb into. "This time," he had said to himself as Daisy's plane taxied down the runway towards the spectators' gallery, "I will give up." And he stubbed out the newly lighted cigarette on the floor.

'Daisy gave him a very warm welcoming kiss and just as he was about to tell her of his new resolution she presented him with a carton of cigarettes. Never before had she given him a light, let alone a cigarette – and she was uncommonly *nice*. The details of her trip, however, were vague. From such a precise woman this was disturbing. Then there was the odd phone call to someone called Simon and a postcard came from Mombassa, Kenya, with the words "Never forget. S."

'Dick confronted Daisy. He told her he knew she was having an affair. The reply was level and direct. Daisy was a good-looking woman and constantly used the mirror to see how her arguments became her. The reflection in the wardrobe's looking glass showed truth in all its majestic righteousness. Daisy was a leading member of the local church and often read the lesson with the same open candour that she now addressed to her reflection.

' "Typical," she sighed in double. "Why can't you men ever realise that women can have wonderful yet platonic relationships? Why is the smallest innocent action blown up into a mountain of sexual activity just to satisfy your fantasies? Simon happens to be a very lovely person who has just arrived in Nairobi as a

17

missionary.'' Here she paused. In between straightening a stray coil back into her blonde beautifully combed hair she had caught sight of Dick's face with incredulity written all over it. Surely not a missionary! He imagined him in that position calling out to whatever God he stood for, as he and Daisy rejoiced and alleluia-ed together. Just as Dick thought he had the advantage, the moral high ground was taken by Daisy as she accused him of Extra Sensory Gutter Perception.

'Not much was mentioned again. The signs were still there but the cloak of sainthood became like armour around Daisy. Dick was angry and impotent. Daisy went frequently to church and made more trips to Nairobi. Mummy and Papa were selling their house and needed a daughter's helping hand.

'It was after one of these trips that Dick found a stack of airmail letters, the type that are made of lightweight paper, pre-stamped and folded to post. A round dozen. Dick took care to count them. The next day there were eleven. Dick casually asked Daisy if she had written to anyone. ''No,'' was the reply. ''To whom should I be writing?'' ''I don't know – you have been known to write letters from time to time.'' ''I suppose your extra senses tell you I have been scribbling letters but are not accurate enough to say to whom.'' The window reflected the pearls round her elegant neck as Daisy twisted them about her slim fingers. She only looked away from her image when she heard Dick explaining that he had counted the letters. Nothing to do with Extra Sensory Perception. ''You've taken to spying on me have you? Well it so happens that I wrote to mummy. It slipped my mind.'' With that she left Dick with his list of chores and drove off to see friends and play tennis at the club.

'Dick thought a quick visit to the local pub would allow him to find a tinge of self respect in a pint of bitter. As he looked for some loose change, which he knew to be

Love and Disharmony

---

behind their wedding photograph showing Daisy's parents in deep mourning over their daughter's choice of a husband, Dick discovered yet another postcard. It was a picture of the sun setting over Mount Kilimanjaro. Written on the back was the message, "I pray the snows will melt again." Surely they hadn't gone to Kilimanjaro and done it in the snow?

'Another letter had gone from the pile of airmail letters. Evidently Daisy had used the stack as a pad. The impression of the ball-point pen showed on the top letter. Carefully Dick took a soft-lead pencil and rubbed it over the top letter. Quite clearly the writing showed up. It started, "My dearest Darling. Dick still suspects but is so gullible that after he huffed and puffed he has accepted everything I have told him. He really is so stupid." The "so stupid" was underlined. The letter then went on to reminisce in graphic detail what they had done (and the missionary position was not the only one) and how much they were going to accomplish in whatever temple of love they would next meet.

'In the following hours Dick struggled with his emotions and his desire to strangle her. He came to the conclusion that he didn't hate her. He just didn't like her very much. Should he walk out? Daisy had made a very comfortable home. He'd miss that. Teach her a lesson? Let her car tyres down? Put soap in her toothpaste? No. Revenge must be sweet and a dish to be eaten as hot as curry.

'Daisy arrived back in a very good mood that lasted as far as the kitchen. Why wasn't the table laid? The salad prepared? What had Dick been doing all afternoon? Dick said nothing for a while and then when Daisy paused for breath, as she caught sight of her glorious self in the oven door, he started. "My dearest Darling," he began.

She sighed. "Oh, you're not going to start all that again are you?" But her voice trailed away as Dick, unrelentingly, quoted on and on. Line for line the letter she had just posted to her lover thousands of miles away. Written and then posted immediately. Yet here was her husband speaking every word she had written from her passionate heart. Her legs gave way and she sank to the floor. Her eyes glazed over and dribble dropped from her slack mouth. How? How? How?

'Dick's revenge was complete. Daisy never learned how he knew her innermost thoughts and spoke them aloud. To her it was total magic. She never again doubted his ability to read minds and his mystical perception. It was the fear that Dick could see into her mind that kept her from ever straying again and she became his devoted servant for the rest of their married life.'

– *with thanks to Robert Young, film director.*

∞

'The late mother of an extremely close friend of ours decided she had had enough of her husband's philandering, but not of her husband. So she decided to call the bluff of his latest squeeze who, it seemed, was fairly determined to lead him to the altar. She telephoned the hapless harpie and invited her to tea at the Ritz. Tea and cakes arrived and the atmosphere was cool but dignified as the conversation turned to the matter in hand.

'Yes, she did love him and wanted to marry him, said the mistress, and nothing would deter her. Our friend's mother smiled sweetly, said she completely understood and that she would drop off their two children with all their belongings at the weekend.

'For some inexplicable reason the erring husband returned to the marital home pretty pronto where they all lived happily ever after.'

– *with thanks to Willie Christie, film director.*

∞

It was a disgusting winter's evening and Dai Llewellyn was driving the gorgeous Gerda Schiller through the underpass at Hyde Park corner towards Tramp. As he drove, he mused over how he was going to break the bad news to Gerda – it was 'Dear John' time. At Tramp he suggested that they 'take it easy for six weeks'. He told her that he would drive her back to his flat: she could sleep there, he would sleep at his brother's place and, the following day, he would sort out somewhere for her to live.

Good as his word, the next day he found a flat and returned home to get Gerda and her bags. As he opened the door it was clear that she had not packed. An empty whisky bottle lay ominously on the floor. Suddenly, she appeared, growling in her distinctive accent: 'Here is yours, baby,' and pointing a 12-bore at his chest. It was Dai's good fortune that she did not know about the safety catch.

A week later, a picture of Dai appeared in a newspaper. He had been to a fancy dress party as the Midnight Cowboy, wearing cowboy gear on top and stockings and suspenders underneath, with a .45 Magnum replica gun in his holster. Someone had decided to report Dai to the Police Anti-Terrorist Squad who duly arrived on his doorstep with three or four squad cars. Only after several hours of serious interrogation were they satisfied that he was not a threat to public safety and that the gun was, indeed, a replica. 'There may be no connection between the two incidents,' said Dai, 'but the inspector in charge of the raid told me at a subsequent meeting that the informant had been female – with a pronounced foreign accent.'

Sexual Subterfuge

— ∞ —

Heav'n has no rage, like love to hatred turn'd,
Nor Hell a fury, like a woman scorn'd.'
William Congreve, *Love for Love*

Sexual Subterfuge

'I was going out with a young lady. One Saturday night we were having a few drinks together in the pub. She went to the ladies and when she came back she accused me of chatting up the barmaid. Later, we returned to my flat in Putney.

'When I woke up the following morning, I was distinctly uncomfortable in the nether regions. I couldn't think what was the matter. I looked around and my girlfriend was nowhere to be seen. Then I spied a note, beside which was a chilli pepper. The note informed me that she had rubbed the pepper on my willy and had stuck a little bit up my backside. I spent the whole of Sunday in the bath, trying to take the heat out of my punishment.'
– *with thanks to Peter Dean, actor.*

∞

A couple lived together for a while until he replaced her with a younger model. The jilted lady was sad that they never had the catharsis of a final row, to which she attributes the following behaviour.

Some time after he had moved out, her lover came back to her place to collect his things and there ensued that horrible sharing of the spoils: these are my CDs, those are your Orwells, you're welcome to those stinking shoes etc. While he was going through the bathroom cabinet she noticed his briefcase sitting,

innocently, in the drawing room. In it, she discovered his passport. She took it out, and a biro and, in the 'Any Distinguishing Features' section she found herself writing 'No Penis'. Knowing that no one ever looks at their own passport, she still takes immense satisfaction from imagining the looks of pity he must get every time he goes through customs.
– *with thanks to A A Gill.*

∞

One hot afternoon at the end of a particularly unsuccessful visit to Windsor Races, a regular punter found himself with only a fiver to get back to the railway station. He approached the only cab on the rank and asked the fare to the station. 'Fifteen quid,' said the surly cabbie.

The punter offered the fiver with the promise to pay the balance on his next visit. The cabbie's reply was succinct and to the point: 'F--- Off.' So the punter was forced to walk all the way to the station; miles and miles in the blazing sun.

Some weeks later the same punter had a gloriously successful afternoon at the Windsor track and, emerging from the course, saw that the same surly cabbie was third in line on the rank.

The punter approached the first cab and asked the driver: 'How much to the station?'

'Fifteen quid, Guv,' came the prompt reply.

The punter leaned into the cab and asked sotto voce: 'How about another twenty quid for a blow-job?'

The furious cabbie shook his fist at him and called him a filthy pervert. The punter good-naturedly approached the second cab on the rank. The same question provoked the same sort of response: 'Nob off you twisted git!'

With a shrug, the punter approached his old adversary

of weeks before. 'How much to the station?' he asked quietly.

'Still fifteen quid,' replied the cabbie.

'Fine,' said the punter and hopped inside.

As they pulled away from the rank the punter leant out of the open cab window, caught the attention of the first two cabbies, winked knowingly and gave them a gleeful thumbs-up. As their jaws dropped he knew that they would never see their colleague in the same light again.

– with thanks to Christopher Wilkins, writer.

∞

Joan found out that her husband was up to no good. She carried on a bold pretence of knowing nothing about the affair but put itching powder in his underpants. After several days he became so worried about his scratching that he thought he had a sexually-transmitted disease and confessed all to his wife.

∞

A Royal Marine was training in Northern Norway. On a dark, November night he went to a discotheque where he met a vision of Scandinavian beauty. Despite the language barrier they managed to communicate and she indicated that it would be a good idea if he went back to her place.

The following morning he awoke at 8 a.m. and, looking around the sparsely furnished bedroom, he wondered where he was. He smiled as it all came back to him but came down to earth with a terrific bump when he looked around. He saw that he had no clothes, no shoes, no wallet – everything had gone – and so had the girl. They must have been stolen. Groaning, he grabbed the telephone and phoned the camp to explain the situation. Having been advised what to do, he thought he would get his own back by leaving a little memento. He climbed

in the middle of the bed – and crapped. Just then his Scandinavian beauty came back in, with all his clothes most beautifully laundered and ironed and his shoes polished to perfection.

∞

The summer heat was unbearable and the traffic in Milan had ground to a halt. AC Milan was playing at home and noisy football supporters were everywhere. A young couple had been crammed on a slow train among football supporters, and were now stuck in a taxi: immobile amongst the stationary cars in the searing temperatures. They were running desperately late for an evening function, but they still had to get back to their hotel somehow and change. Their tempers were running high.

Now came the final straw: he absolutely insisted on stopping for a drink. No, he couldn't wait until they got back to the hotel. The queue at the street café seemed endless but he was adamant – he had an absolute fixation about having a grapefruit juice. She stayed in the car and fumed as he got out to join the queue.

'Oh, what's the Italian for a grapefruit juice?' he asked.

'Pompino, uno pompino,' she replied innocently.

Her mood lifted in anticipation of coming events. Eventually he got to the front of the queue. 'Pompino, per favore,' he shouted above the noise to the pretty teenage girl behind the bar. The queue of burly football supporters broke up and collapsed with laughter as did his wife. The Italian for grapefruit is 'pompelmo'. He had just asked for a blow job.

∞

When London's most confirmed bachelor announced he was going to get married, his friends could hardly

believe it. A rampant sexist, racist and homophobe, he loved his bachelor ways and prided himself that he always had a bevy of beautiful babes on his arms and in his bed. He was positively looking forward to the inevitable stripper he would get on his stag night.

However, he had also been the instigator of some appalling behaviour at all his friends' stag parties so they decided to give him a stag party to end all stag parties and get their revenge for past deeds. Their research led them to 'one of those agencies' and the gentleman at the other end of the telephone was most helpful, asking after his particular preferences and peccadilloes.

'I've got just the person for you: black; ugly as sin; arrives, undresses the "victim", ties him to the table in front of everyone; administers a perfect "Hugh Grant special" and then does a slow striptease. If you blindfold your friend before the grand entrance, he'll get a lovely surprise afterwards.'

'Sounds perfect,' said the lads. 'How much does she charge?'

The reply was more than they could ever have wished for: 'Oh, don't worry, *he* won't charge a thing.'

∞

Phillip Seldon does not know whether anyone has actually used this revenge, but it has proved a highly popular discussion point with the ladies during his courses. (Phillip runs courses in Manhattan entitled: 'How to Get Even without Breaking the Law', in which he teaches people how to use totally legal and socially acceptable methods of revenge, such as the media, bankruptcy court or even jail. The three-hour course costs $39 – details from Seldon on 001 212 570 6500!)

First, hire a prostitute to pick up your ex-man – any

bar or meeting place will do; just make it look casual. She has been briefed to seduce him and, of course, get him to take off his clothes. Then, when he is naked, relaxed and beginning to enjoy himself, she will point at his 'member' and roar with laughter at how small it is, how bent it is, how thin it is, or whatever his particular hang-up may be.

∞

A man came home early and caught his wife in the act with another man. He led him down to the garden shed, still naked, and took him to the work bench where he put his penis in a vice. He reached for the saw.

'You're, you're not going to . . .?' stammered the interrupted Lothario.

'No, but *you* are!' laughed the cuckold as he set fire to the garden shed.

– with thanks to Jethro, the famous Cornish comedian.

∞

A woman planned her revenge on her boyfriend and his best mate very carefully. She arranged to meet them in a bar one Saturday night with the objective of 'getting ripped'. They had an endless succession of Tequila Slammers but the boys did not realise she had a prior arrangement with the barman and that the colourless liquid in her glass was, in fact, water. By the time they left they were completely brainless and they weaved their way back to her place for a nightcap, after which both chaps collapsed in a stupor.

She managed to drag both of the passed-out forms to her big double bed. She stripped them both naked, put them into bed together and scrubbed their private parts, front and back, with a toothbrush until they were red and raw. Then she made herself scarce. The boys woke the next morning, badly hungover, naked in bed with

each other and with very sore parts. She left it to them to work out what had happened.

∞

Piers Adam is a man with a successful chain of restaurants and a well-developed sense of humour. One of his best friends is top photographer Bob Carlos Clarke and the two of them are always playing tricks on each other. Sometimes these get a little out of hand.

The first Piers knew about it was when he received a letter on the letterhead of a well-known private hospital saying:

Dear Mr Adams,
Miss Emily Oppenheimer has asked us to contact you directly having recently visited our outpatients department for tests.
Unfortunately these tests have proved positive and Miss Oppenheimer is concerned that you have transmitted the infection to her as you have been her only sexual partner. It is most important that you should submit yourself for testing without delay. In the meantime you should not engage in any further sexual activity with any partners of either sex and, in order to reduce the spread of infection, please forward us a list of all your sexual contacts during the past eight years.
Please do not panic. It is possible that you are not a carrier and, even if you are, recent medical advances have vastly improved the treatments and life-expectancy of sufferers. If necessary, our counsellors will be available to explain the nature of your illness.
    Yours sincerely,
      Dr A Scholes.

Our hero was petrified. He spent a day arranging his funeral and putting his business in order. He telephoned the hospital to contact Dr A Scholes but they had no record of him, nor had any of its sister hospitals. After forty-eight hours of cold sweat and tears, he worked out that his dear friend Bob was behind this. Right, he thought. Photographers use models. Time for revenge.

Piers managed to get some letterhead from one of the UK's top model agencies and invented a story to get his own back on Bob. His letter read:

> *Dear Bob,*
> *I have been informed about allegations that have been made about you concerning a sexual assault on one of our models, Sophie Anderton, on a recent shoot. Obviously we have to take this matter seriously and I believe that the police have been informed so that they can make their own inquiries. I do hope that this matter can be resolved quickly so that your reputation need not be tarnished more than necessary.*
> *Yours sincerely,*
> *. . .*

This was followed up with a solicitor's letter informing him of criminal proceedings.

Unfortunately, the correspondence went to the wrong studio where it was leaked to the press and what started as a merry joke between friends was to become a living nightmare for both Bob and Piers.

The first Bob knew of it was when a group of paparazzi arrived outside his darkroom. The phones started ringing and the world's press were on to the story – the private joke had become a public concern – 'the world-famous photographer and the under-age model.' Bad enough if it is true but far worse if it is nothing but a joke gone wrong. The *News of The World* wanted to run the story and it took the combined efforts of Piers, Bob and a barrage of solicitors and injunctions to prove it was nothing but a hoax.

– with thanks to Piers Adam and Bob Carlos Clarke for letting us use the story.

∞

Oh, how she wanted to get her revenge on her husband but they were *both* caught out hook, line and sinker. He telephoned her to say he would be back very late that evening as he was in a meeting with Peter Taylor and would be going out afterwards. She knew he wasn't telling the truth. Peter Taylor was lying next to her in bed.

∞

A sexy Soviet was treated in hospital for swelling and inflammation. His wife had discovered he was being unfaithful and found a condom hidden in one of his pockets. She carefully opened it, put in a little ground pepper, resealed it and slipped it back into its hiding place.

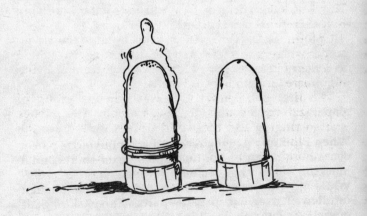

∞

When Phillippa Arugez received an anonymous parcel containing a pair of her husband's boxer shorts and a mocking note, she decided revenge was in order. While he was asleep, she poured a pan of molten candlewax over his private parts. Three skin graft operations later he decided that the marriage had run its course.

∞

The other diners in the restaurant were, as one does, trying to look as though they were taking no notice but at the same time hanging on to every word of the arguing couple in their midst. Even the most stoic among them could not contain their mirth at the grand finale.

When the girl got up to leave the man unzipped his fly, pulled out what could only be described as a whopper, plonked it on the table and cried, 'Well, you won't be wanting any more of *this* then I presume.' Exit one very red-faced ex-lover.

Nasty Neighbours

— ∞ —

A man that studieth revenge keeps his own
wounds green.'

Francis Bacon, *The Essays*

Nasty Neighbours

An uneasy peace reigned between two neighbours in a genteel and leafy part of Ealing. Their mutual loathing was no secret in the area and there had always been feuding over the exact position of the dustbins, the positioning of cars when parked and endless problems over noise and boundary walls. The relative tranquillity was shattered in spring when the crocuses came up. They had been planted in formation to read: 'We hate the Bartletts'.

∞

Following a blazing row over a skateboard which ended years of friendship, a woman plotted revenge against the couple next door. For nearly two years she bombarded them with junk mail, sending off forms from newspapers and magazines filled in with their names, and blitzing them with mail order catalogues, booklets, information on double glazing, conservatories, book clubs and music clubs. Salesmen plagued them day and night, representatives arrived on their doorstep and a steady stream of goods had to be sent back. The final straw came when the victims found that they were being blacklisted as time-wasters and bad debtors by credit companies.

∞

The Rt Hon the Lord Stafford became upset when Beech Caves, at his home in Staffordshire, were continually being used for rave parties. In order to stop them he had fourteen tons of pig slurry dumped in the mouth of the cave. The ravers had the last laugh – what he hadn't realised was that the cave was directly upwind of his mother's house. She had a large houseparty at the time and was distinctly unamused.

∞

In Natick, Massachusetts, outside Boston, two neighbours had settled into a regular and lifelong feud. They deliberately upset each other and things finally came to a head. The wife in the yellow house went to answer the doorbell one day and was nearly shocked to death to find an undertaker, who had come, he said, to collect the body of her husband whom she had believed to be alive and well – and at work. She genuinely believed he must have been killed on his way to the office.

Some time after this nasty event their neighbours received an entire truckload of wet cement on their doorstep. Unfortunately it had dried before they discovered it.

∞

A good Christian was always picking fights with his Jewish neighbour so, in retaliation against the gentile, the Jew sent him a card at Easter saying: 'I'm sorry we killed your God.'

∞

Deep in East Sussex two neighbours lived in peace and friendship . . . until the dog at 24 ate the rabbit at 26. It was four years before the neighbours spoke to each other again.

Came the time of number 26's daughter's sixteenth birthday and the people at number 24 bought her a huge box of chocolates – she was a chubby little thing and renowned for her sweet tooth. They were having drinks

together, and the 24s handed over their present with a few well-chosen words about how glad they were that they were all friends again. The birthday girl opened her present and, to their horror, they saw it was a box of chocolate bunnies. They truly had not realised when they bought it.

They had to move house two months later because relations became so bad.

Road Hogs

— ∞ —

'He meditates revenge who least complains.'
John Dryden, 1631–1700

Road Hogs

The blonde was clearly wearing nothing under her fine silk shirt and Susie's fiancé could not take his eyes off her. Throughout dinner in the top London restaurant Caviar Kaspia, Susie had a lovely view of his back as he talked animatedly to the blonde and shared endless vodkas. Later, in Annabel's, he danced and laughed with her for hours. Susie ordered a bottle of the most expensive champagne on the wine list and put it on his bill, but even that did not bring him back down to earth – he continued to flirt and ignore her totally. As she sat at the table, Susie plotted how to get her own back.

When it finally came to their departure, she smiled sweetly at him and said she'd had rather a lot to drink – would he mind driving home? She knew he had had far more to drink than she had. She also knew that one of his brake lights was not working, which greatly increased his chances of being stopped by the police. She chuckled to herself when she saw the blue flashing light in the rear-view mirror . . .

∞

A bus timetable clerk had encouraged drivers to run ahead of schedule, persuading them to go faster so that he could quit early and meet his girlfriend, but the inspector stopped him. To get his own back the clerk sent the inspector seven tons of horse manure, an undertaker with a hearse, a lorry-load of ready-mixed concrete, a repairman to deal with a fictitious gas leak and three tons of anthracite. He also sent a scrap merchant to collect a wrecked car from him and placed a newspaper advertisement to sell the inspector's car. Unfortunately, this sweet revenge resulted in the clerk being sent to jail for two months.

∞

A certain well-known rock 'n' roll star was waiting for a taxi in the Cromwell Road. It was a damp and unpleasant evening and he was delighted to see a comforting yellow light on an approaching cab. To his horror, a gaggle of American tourists who had been watching him waiting in the rain leapt out of a doorway ten yards ahead of him and flagged down his cab.

It stopped for them. The star approached the cab to protest but the Americans already had the door open. As he arrived one of them turned to him and drawled: 'Say, do you know which *thee-a-ter* is showing *The Mousetrap*?' 'Yes,' he replied, 'It's at the St Martin's Theatre. Oh, and by the way, the – – – did it.'
(– *culprit's name removed to preserve this great mystery!*)

∞

Some time ago a farmer in the West Country had been involved in a lengthy battle with the council – letters had been going back and forth for over a year about planning permissions yet he was getting nowhere. Finally, enough was enough. He loaded up his slurry tanker – a machine used to propel breathtakingly smelly semi-liquid clods of animal waste on to fields as fertiliser. He drove to the council offices and sprayed this organic matter all over the front of the building. He was subsequently fined but in a television interview said that it was worth every penny of the fine he had to pay in order to let the council know what he thought of them.

Stop press! We have recently heard that the same man

54

was in dispute with his bank about overdraft charges — and, you guessed it, they too became the beneficiaries of a truckload of manure.

∞

When the recession really bit in the late Eighties, leading to the virtual extinction of the yuppie, a lot of city boys lost their jobs with immediate effect. It became fairly common practice, when asked to return the company car (a Porsche, of course), to leave it on a double yellow line outside the office, collecting parking tickets and wheel clamps, while the bosses tried in vain to locate the keys. The ex-employees would simply have chucked them down the nearest drain.

∞

As the final shot of their long-running battle, a jilted woman drove her ex-boyfriend's car to Heathrow and parked it in the short-term car park where the charge is £1.80 per hour. It was three weeks before she told him where it was – nearly £1,000 later.

∞

A rejected Romeo was found guilty of endangering life and of drink and driving offences when he took revenge on the girl by driving a car at her house. He was so drunk that he missed the house and hit the one next door.

∞

'I am glad I owned up and, although I know I did the wrong thing, I am not ashamed.' So said a council executive's wife, adding that men should take heed of the fact that women are less prepared now to sit back without retaliating. 'We are less frightened of our feelings and expressing them. There are going to be more cases like this,' she said. And the reason for her revenge?

Infidelity, of course. She decided to act when her husband continued to live and sleep with her, whilst carrying on an affair with a business colleague. She discovered that he was with his lover. 'I saw his Mercedes outside (which I had chosen).' Using her spare key she got into the car and, with her Irish Wolfhound at her side, drove to the Town Hall. She aimed the car at the large, plate-glass doors, revved the engine, took off the handbrake and accelerated forward, smashing the doors to smithereens. She then reversed the car and drove to the sea wall, where she planned to drive the car into the sea. 'But there was a man fishing so I just dumped it,' she said. The intrepid duo then ran home. She was already down as a suspect when she owned up to the Police two days later. 'I feel a lot better,' she told them.

∞

It was slowly becoming a living nightmare as Annabel Hornby started to realise that her husband's affections seemed to be greater for his beloved car than they were for her. The car certainly took up more of his time. One of them had to go and it was not going to be Annabel. She took a space in *Loot* advertising the sale of her husband's car for just £10. She was slightly surprised when no responses were forthcoming. However, after a second week of advertising, a student turned up at her door and could not believe his luck when he exchanged a £10 note for an extremely valuable, genuine Ferrari.

∞

There are just under 30,000 policemen in London and around about the same number of cabbies. Usually an atmosphere of peace and cooperation prevails between the two but, occasionally, the one has to get the other back in line. Under the old Hackney Carriage Act a number of laws govern cabbies. Amongst other requirements, they are

duty-bound to hand in any lost property to the police.

One cabbie tells of a period of time when they were frequently being harassed at a particular taxi rank: the police continually moved them up and gave them a hard time about causing obstruction. For a month, each and every cabbie familiar with that rank waged a campaign to get their own back. They handed in every item of lost property found in their cabs, including empty cigarette packets and newspapers, and we're told that some of the more enthusiastic cabbies went through the rubbish to find broken umbrellas, old macs and discarded bags which were duly handed in. It was not long before an amnesty was called and peace reigned once more.

∞

It was Christmas time and a young couple were on their way back from a drinks party, driving through the country lanes of Kent. Oh-oh, they thought, seeing the blue flashing light behind them; time to pull over. A policeman approached the side window. 'Excuse me, Sir, have you been drinking?' 'Yes,' beamed the occupant. 'May I ask how much, Sir?' said the policeman. 'Certainly: four, no, maybe five whiskies,' he replied. Suddenly the policeman became officious and started reading the man his rights. 'But . . . officer, you don't . . .' he stammered, trying to get a word in edgeways, to no avail: the policeman was having none of it. The occupant was not a vindictive man but was incensed by the policeman's rudeness. Right, he thought, have it your way. I'll get you back for your brusqueness.

The policeman ordered the man out of the car and asked him to blow into the bag. When he had finished the man handed the bag to the policeman, who smugly told him by how many units he was over the limit and asked him if he had anything to say. 'Yes,' he said indignantly. 'My wife hasn't had a drop. This is a left-hand-drive car and *she* is driving.'

∞

The owner of a successful lorry driving and mobile cement mixer business was concerned that his wife was having an affair. He slipped home during the day, only to have his worst fears confirmed: the curtains upstairs were drawn and there was a convertible red sports car on the road outside. 'I'll soon fix that!' he thought as he tipped the entire contents of his cement mixture into the open car. Shortly afterwards his front door opened and the family doctor emerged and drove off in his blue Sierra. He had, quite simply, been making a house call. The red car belonged to a total stranger.

∞

The wealthy boss of the car wash was very particular about his 911 Porsche. It had to be gleaming when he arrived for work and someone had to be sure it had been put through the wash for him, irrespective of his time of arrival. One morning, the boss arrived earlier than usual for work and the car had not been cleaned, so the hapless lackey responsible was fired. The lackey was very miffed about this so, on his last day of employment, he went into the car wash and secretly fixed hidden wire coat hangers inside those oh-so-soft washing brushes that rub the car clean . . .

∞

The local GP finally had enough of the shoppers and trippers who would arrive in the charming village of Chipping Campden, open their car doors and let out their dogs who would immediately evacuate themselves, usually right outside his home or surgery. He quite simply scooped up the offending mess with a trowel and popped it back in the car.

∞

A man wanted to get back at the appliance repair firm which promised five times in a twelve-hour period that the repair man was on his way – he made thousands of phoney coupons offering a free microwave service and put them on the windshields of all the cars parked near the company.

A woman in Chicago glued sand on to her detestable brother-in-law's windscreen wipers. It made lovely designs on the windscreen.

Office Politics

—— ∞ ——

'If you are in the business of revenge
– then you had better dig two graves.'
                              Chinese proverb

Office Politics

The flamboyant head of a large London advertising agency always wore casual clothes to the office in a vain attempt to pass himself off as 'one of the lads'. However, he always kept an expensive designer suit hanging on the back of his office door, in case of an emergency meeting with important clients.

He only made three wrong career moves in his life. The first was to have an indiscreet and long-running affair with his secretary. The second was to dump her publicly and unceremoniously in favour of an eighteen-year-old temp in the Accounts Department. And the third was to order the same long-suffering secretary to take his 'emergency' suit to the cleaners in readiness for an early morning presentation to the Ministry of Defence when the agency stood a good chance of being awarded the highly lucrative naval recruitment account.

She duly obeyed his instructions, omitting to mention a refinement which he only discovered twenty minutes before the presentation was due to take place. She had arranged with the dry cleaners that the trousers were shortened by eight inches.

∞

When Mr Smith discovered his wife was having an affair with her boss he decided to exact spectacular revenge. In order to do so he carefully researched and collected data and information on the eminent international firm where she worked.

First he sent tapes and letters to all the senior executives at his wife's office, informing them of his wife's affair with their chief executive. Not content with this, he then hacked into the firm's computer and wrote an embarrassingly frank memo in his wife's name, to be distributed around the company. Not only did it admit to the affair but also gave intimate details about key staff and company directors. Her private life 'she' said was a disaster and had been 'virtually sexless' for seven years. The memo went on to suggest that there were to be many redundancies and that 'several senior staff are not justifying their enormous salaries'.

He then sent the tapes and letters to the executive's wife, who said that 'it came like a bolt out of the blue'. Having been confronted by *his* wife, the lover admitted the affair and was promptly asked to leave the family home. He is no longer chief executive and is now in an overseas office. Mrs Smith resigned the day after the letter was sent out.

∞

A now-eminent solicitor assures us that this was not his idea. He had just joined the firm as articled clerk and his senior assistant solicitors devised a gentle revenge to put a rather tedious man in his place.

This fellow had never arrived late for work, neither had he been off sick in thirty years. He would arrive at the office at 9.26 a.m., remove his bowler hat and hang it on the rack. When he left at 5.31 p.m. it was on with the bowler and off into the night. The lads did some homework. They examined the hat, procured an identical one but a couple of sizes smaller and effected an exchange with that of their victim. He left that evening and was not seen the following day.

The boys in the office did not find out until later but the man was greatly puzzled and went to his doctor

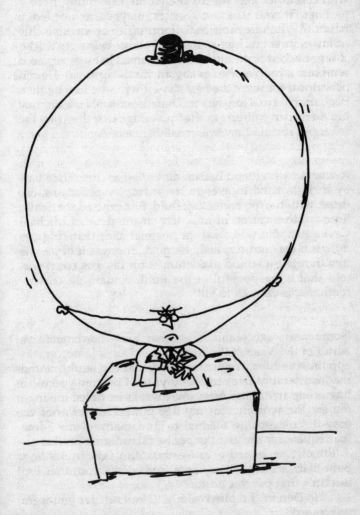

who could not explain his incredible expanding head – perhaps it was the weather or maybe he needed a haircut? When he came back to the office he gave no clue of his trauma but was well teased about being off work.

Stage two was put into play. The small hat was replaced with one a couple of sizes *larger* than the original. He did not appear for work the next day either as he had by then been referred to a consultant. The lads returned the original hat thereafter, but safe in the knowledge that they had the other two should they ever need them again.

∞

A woman who heard herself described as 'the office tart' by a clerk, tried to avenge the insult by poisoning his drink with typing correcting fluid. She poured the white liquid into a carton of milk left on the desk of Michael Cavendish. He was taken to hospital after drinking the milk but was not seriously harmed. She was lucky – she had thought it would make him 'a bit ill'. The court was told that a teaspoonful of the fluid, containing trichloroethane, is enough to kill.

∞

'Some years ago – and in another life – I was features editor of the *News of the World*, when Derek Jameson was appointed editor. We did not get on. He, no doubt, found me insufferably arrogant. I found his Cockney yo-ho-ho bogus and irritating. After some weeks he called me in to review the workings of my department. It was not an easy discussion; he seemed to find many of my ideas inadequate for the great paper he intended to produce.

'Finally, he leaned over his desk and said in his best Bow Bells accent: "You know Rod, don't you, that I'm Britain's first psychic editor?"

' "No Derek," I replied calmly. "I had no idea you were so blessed."

' "Oh yes," he said, warming to his theme. "My Ellen (his wife) and I, we're both psychic. I can tell when things are going to happen. I knew I was going to get this job, 'cos I'm psychic, see? 'Course I got the timing wrong – psychics do that – I thought I was going to get it a year ago when it went to Asker. But I knew it was coming. What do you think of that?"

' "Very interesting," I said, as non-committally as possible. But all the time I was thinking: "Oh, no! I've just had a year working for a tricky editor. Now I've got a psychic one."

'He interrupted my reverie: "And, you know, Rod," he said, "being psychic, like I am, I can see us not getting on."

'I left the paper about a month later – and have not regretted it one bit since. Derek lasted a bit longer; but, in the end, the circulation continued to tumble and he, too, left suddenly.

'The day he went, I sent him a postcard. It was addressed to Derek Jameson (Britain's First Psychic Editor) and it said: "Pity you didn't see it coming." '
– *with thanks to Rod Tyler.*

∞

A major TV executive summoned a junior editing hack and insisted that a particular current affairs programme, which had been transmitted very late the previous night, must be 're-edited' for a showing at the board meeting the following day. The young-but-enthusiastic editor protested, but was advised that, unless the major exec's will was followed, his neck would be on the line.

The programme had been broadcast 'live' and contained complicated errors involving high level corporate policy which were potentially explosive to the executive's career. The young editor discovered the major gaffe in the programme and realised that it was the responsibility of the major executive. The young blade decided to exact his revenge – he duly spent many hours editing the programme as requested and this was shown to the board at the appointed hour.

After the event the major exec called in the junior to say well done. 'Would all the board like a copy as a keepsake?' the editor asked. The major exec thought this a wonderful idea and urged junior on. Which copy of the tape do you think the board received in their mail the following day?

∞

In Weston-Super-Mare a small but successful confectionery factory produced lettered rock which is familiar at all British seaside resorts. This particular factory, Farmiloe's, owned and run by Mrs Farmiloe herself many years ago, employed an unpopular foreman whose job it was to oversee the time-honoured procedure of putting the coloured rods around the outside of the huge fat, round block of rock and inserting the letter rods in the middle before they were stretched into the long, thin sticks that we know and love.

The foreman finally earned himself the sack for one too many transgressions and, before he left, he decided to create a little souvenir of his time at the factory. He rearranged the letters to create around ten miles of rock bearing the message: 'Get Stuffed Mrs Farmiloe.'

∞

A junior medic was given punishment duties at the hospital and a senior spokesman said: 'We didn't think it was funny.' The medic's 'crime'? A woman spent ten days on the loo after he had laced her cup of tea with the world's most powerful laxative – the potent drug 'Picolax'. She was his nursing boss and had moaned about his work. Pauline Ainsworth lost pounds before the effects of the prescription-only drug wore off.

70

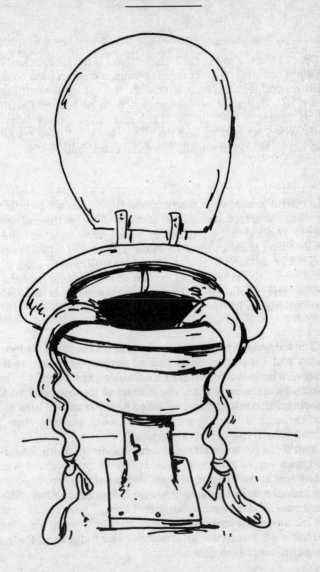

∞

A peer of the realm is now rather careful what he eats since he went stalking with, amongst others, a cordon bleu cook with a grudge. Lunch time saw the hungry peer settling down to a delicious venison stew which he finished with relish, much to the hilarity of the rest of the house party. Only when he had picked the plate clean did they reveal that his stew was made entirely from stags' balls.

∞

A man in New York needed to pay back a manager in his office who was always playing practical jokes on people. He took a styrofoam plate and filled it with cottage cheese and other perishable food. He then covered the whole thing with another styrofoam plate and taped it up under her desk so that she would be unlikely to find it. For months the smell bothered her and it was six months before she found the 'Blue Plate Special'. It caused pandemonium in the office when she opened it.

∞

C O Stanley was the notoriously tough chairman of Pye Radio and TV in the 1950s and all employees knew that anyone who put a foot out of line was out of a job.

John Hodgeson was in the statistical department and answered the telephone one day. A voice asked him to run through some figures which took quite a time, during which the tea trolley arrived.

'You'll have to wait; the tea trolley is here,' said Hodgeson.

'Do you know who it is here?' boomed a voice.

Suddenly realising who it was, Hodgeson replied: 'Do you know who *you* are talking to?'

'No!' came the strangled reply.

'That's all I wanted to know!' said Hodgeson, slamming the telephone down.

∞

After two weeks in his office a temp had had quite enough of her boss. She appreciated that there was a certain anonymity to being a temp but she felt he really didn't need to treat her like an automaton/workhorse. He was particularly keen on time-keeping and made it clear that she should not go to the loo in his time, nor waste one second of his time, ever.

On her final day he went out to lunch, leaving her with a pile of work which 'must be finished before you leave'. OK, she thought, but before she got down to it she decided she would have a little fun with his diary. She cancelled some lunches, erased a few meetings and rearranged others.

She subsequently heard from her replacement of the devastation she left in her wake, as he turned up in Huddersfield for a meeting with a man who wasn't there; he waited in restaurants in vain; and left his mornings clear for meetings which simply did not happen.
– *with thanks to the Hon. Dickon Kindersley.*

∞

A senior government minister was an excellent orator, thanks entirely to a civil servant who wrote all his speeches. So reliable was the material that the minister was able to stand and deliver his words without ever rehearsing them. The civil servant, however, was more than a little disgruntled that the minister had never had the courtesy to thank him so he decided to get his own back.

Came the day of an important keynote speech and the minister took his place on the podium. He was moving the audience to new heights with his winning words when he turned the page and, to his horror, saw the words: 'You're on your own, you bugger!'
– *with thanks to Michael Grade.*

∞

During the late 1970s, the teetering Labour Government, while operating without an overall parliamentary majority, was ruled with a rod of iron by Deputy Chief Whip Walter Harrison, MP for Wakefield. At a time when every vote was crucial he cracked the whip to make members show up and vote – he never missed a transgression and he never forgot a kindness. An MP was once absent for a vote and Walter discovered that he was in Crete. 'Aye, and when the bastard gets back he'll be in bloody concrete,' exploded the Whip.

On one occasion he encountered a new TV political correspondent in the palace of Westminster. With no warning Harrison's hand reached out and gave the unsuspecting chap a nasty tweak of the balls. The poor man turned to Harrison, ashen faced and doubled up in pain, to hear him say, by way of explanation: 'And that's for nothing. Just imagine what'll happen to you if you ever cross me!'

When the Speaker announces a Division – the Ayes to the Right, the Noes to the Left – there is usually a mad rush and, inevitably, there are late-comers who struggle to get through at the last split second before the doors close. Three sturdy Tory MPs developed a ploy to keep talking in the entrance to the Ayes lobby so that late Labour members would have to dodge and weave and hurdle to get in. Joint consultation did not improve the situation so the Labour Deputy Chief Whip perfectly timed a rugby tackle which threw the three Tory MPs into the Labour Lobby just before the 'door-closing'. Their votes were, therefore, counted *with* the government and this was immediately reported to the press. The three did not repeat their blocking tactics again.

Another time Harrison entered the Strangers' Bar at the House of Commons and friends told him they had left him a 'Thick 'Un' (a double whisky). Harrison raised it to his mouth only to discover it was a trick glass – just a vision in a double-sealed container. Sweet revenge came quickly: the nuts and crisps, which were provided free to customers, were replaced with polystyrene parcel stuffing looking exactly like crisps. He promoted them for consumption to the original jokers telling them they would taste a lot better with sugar on them.

These were times when sick or dying MPs from both sides of the House were brought in by ambulance to vote; so tenuous was the government's hold on power. One evening in 1979 Walter Harrison insisted that one dying Labour MP should stay at home, despite rasping protestations to the contrary. That very night, in a motion of no-confidence, the Labour Government fell – by one single vote. But even today, having had a Conservative Government ever since, Harrison knows that he did the right thing.

– *with thanks to The Rt Hon Walter Harrison, JP.*

∞

'A long time ago I wanted to get into marketing and applied to a huge international company for a job. The person I needed to speak to kept fobbing me off; he refused my calls and never called back. So, I reported him missing to the Police. He called back within ten minutes! Needless to say I didn't get the job; I just got a very angry policeman.

'Years later I was with the chairman of this company. I asked him about this particular minion and whether he was still with the company. He did some research and found out that he had left "in upsetting circumstances". I told him of my encounter and that I could have ended up doing his job. "Oh," inquired the boss, "Would you like the job now?" '

– *with thanks to writer and TV presenter, Jeremy Beadle.*

Little Angels

'Don't get mad: get even!'

Little Angels

The nice young ladies of St Leonard's College exacted their revenge on an unpopular teacher. They got hold of a shop dummy and dressed her in school uniform. The dummy was then suspended by a noose around her neck from an upper window outside this particular teacher's sitting room, during the night. When she opened the curtains the next morning, she had the most horrible shock and had to take the rest of the day off.

∞

The girls at Downe House school were finishing off a midnight feast and wondering what they could do next. They all agreed that the services in Chapel were too dull and that it was time to do something about it. Off they crept, and a couple of brave volunteers climbed up the tower to the bell and wound their dressing gown cords all around it to silence it. The following day the bell ringers pulled like mad to sound the bell that summons the whole school to chapel and . . . silence. Just the headmistress and the organist standing in the chapel, all alone. No chapel that day.

∞

Several children at a famous public school took a cardboard box and cut out the bottom. They then placed it in the middle of the corridor, filled it with twenty mice and taped the top shut knowing that the headmistress was coming along at any minute. The chaos was indescribable when she picked up the box.

∞

The Australian nanny made a good pretence of getting on well with the family. She always had a smile on her face and was friendly and cooperative. Both parents were lawyers and worked hard and while they were at their respective offices she enjoyed sole charge of the children. During the day, when they were at school, the nanny had been asked to clear out all the children's outgrown clothes and all the baby equipment and take them to the second-hand shop, which she sweetly did – the couple had made it clear that they were *definitely* having no more children.

Came a time when the unappreciative couple were going away to a remote Caribbean island, leaving the exhausted nanny and children for two weeks. The couple wanted to crash out in the sun and 'get to know each other again' on a second honeymoon.

As the resentful nanny waved them goodbye she smiled, remembering how she had quietly removed mum's contraceptive pills from her spongebag and hidden them in the bathroom.

∞

'When I was a very young girl at boarding school in Kenya, as in most schools, we had a bully. She was a girl who was older than the rest of us seven-year-olds and took advantage of her position as the oldest in the dormitory. Most of us learned to keep one step ahead of her although none of us escaped the bullying and the blackmail completely.

'One term, a new girl joined the school and she was the perfect target: small in size, very shy, extremely insecure and desperately homesick. She became the main focus of our bully. Needless to say she was totally unable to cope and it was obvious to everyone that if something wasn't done, she would crack. Telling teachers and matrons about this sort of thing never occurred to us, it just wasn't done, so two friends and I planned a campaign.

'All dormitories had their rules set down by matron and if these were broken badly enough the offender was removed to another dormitory. Rule one: all shoes had to be cleaned and put at the end of our beds each morning for inspection; then, after dressing, we were marched to breakfast. In no circumstances must anyone be late for meals. Therefore, my friends and I systematically hid vital bits of uniform and shoes so our bully was regularly late for breakfast, frequently improperly dressed! (Rule two: all girls must wear full uniform at all times other than recreation times.)

Rule three: all homework must be presented on time each morning. Miss X suddenly had trouble locating the homework she had done the previous evening and, therefore, was unable to present it in class – Big Trouble!!

There were several other "magic moments" when we got the better of her. While all this was going on, it distracted her attention and our little friend had time to settle in and adjust to boarding school. To our delight, Miss X was moved to another dormitory the next term where she was to become the subject of some "shall we say, gentle persuasion"!'
– with thanks to Diane Keen, actress.

∞

A couple of decades ago a pupil at Westminster School had had enough of a rather unpleasant bully – a monitor who prided himself on the tidiness and immaculate state of his study. He would strut around ticking off those whose studies were in a mess and set all manner of unsavoury jobs as punishment. Peter decided to get his own back.

He asked matron for some bread to feed the birds in St James' Park. Matron handed the bread over with an indulgent smile: 'How sweet,' she thought. Peter took his duffle bag and sat on a park bench. The OAPs on either side were evidently as charmed as Matron by this selfless act and he received many smiles of encouragement. The pigeons came closer and closer, strutting and cooing as they fluttered over the bread, and finally actually settled on Peter's arms and hands. Then came the difficult part: catching one without being seen and with minimum noise and loss of feathers. The first was no problem, the second a little more of a struggle.

Back to school he went, straight to the monitor's study where all windows were carefully closed. Bread was scattered liberally, the birds released and the door closed. The devastation after a couple of hours was a sight to behold.

– *with apologies to the RSPB.*

∞

A young lad built up quite a resentment towards a housemaster at school who, he believed, picked on him at every opportunity. The housemaster was due to go away for a few days and asked the boy to feed his dog during his absence to which the boy kindly agreed.

The boy looked after the dog well and, on the night before the master was due back, gave him some chocolate as an extra-special treat. Only it wasn't ordinary chocolate. It was Ex-lax . . .

An Englishman's Home . . .

— ∞ —

'. . . if you wrong us, shall we not revenge?'
William Shakespeare, *The Merchant of Venice*

An Englishman's Home . . .

Fiorella is a beautiful literary agent who was going out with a very promiscuous and big headed racing driver. She could see that the writing was on the wall and, believing that you should never go out without taking a bow, decided to leave him a souvenir of their time together. She spent a whole afternoon cutting up bits of paper with the words 'I love you' written on each one. She put them all over the apartment: in his pockets, in the salt and pepper mills, the bag of flour, in pillow and cushion covers, between the pages of books – there was no end to her creativity.

He was still finding them a year later; he actually phoned her to tell her she had just blown it for him yet again when his current girlfriend found one of her billets-doux.

∞

A couple of plumbers got their own back on the obnoxious home-owners for whom they were working. They plumbed the radiators into the hot-water system, rather than the heating system, which meant the rads were permanently hot . . . perfectly acceptable until the summer came.

∞

A man returned home from work and was somewhat surprised to find that his house was not quite the colour it had been when he left that morning. He had recently dropped his girlfriend and returned to his former love – who happened to be his ex's sister. The jilted sibling had caused £3,149-worth of damage by painting the carpets, furniture and the walls in blue gloss paint; she wrote: 'You will wish you had never messed with me' on the walls; and glued his CD's to their boxes.

The magistrate said that although there had been considerable provocation, they could not send out the message that people could go round doing that sort of thing every time they fell out with their boyfriend. She was bound over to keep the peace for a year and ordered to pay £45 costs.

∞

Althea Barclay was only 18 when she exacted her revenge on Rory Annesley, although she cannot remember what he had done to deserve it.

She let herself into his flat when she knew he was going away for a few days. She turned up the heating, dampened the carpets and sprinkled mustard and cress seeds throughout the flat. A verdant, four-inch deep living carpet greeted his return. Despite this, Althea later became Mrs Rory Annesley.

∞

The divorce was messy and unpleasant and he deeply resented the fact that she stood to gain so much of the empire that he himself had built from scratch long before she had come on the scene. The spoils were being divided and it seemed that there was no end to her demands.

When his lawyer said that the furniture had to be divided in half, something snapped. He had each and every piece of beautiful furniture – French cabinets,

mahogany tables, sofas and armchairs – cut in half down the middle. He even made two matching heaps of sawdust.

∞

In *Pillow Talk*, a 1959 film starring Rock Hudson as playboy Brad Allen and Doris Day as interior designer Jan Morrow, Jan finds out that Brad has been playing with her affections. Jan gets him out of his apartment for a few days and has the entire place redecorated . . . as a bordello.

∞

A certain aristocrat grew increasingly irritated by the hordes of people who, each summer, regarded his garden as a public picnic area. They thought nothing of spreading their blankets and setting up camp right outside his window and, when they had finished, leaving assorted bottles, bags and rubbish scattered all over the lawn.

One party had been particularly obnoxious. As they left, he hastily grabbed a number of things from the larder and threw them in a basket, leapt into his car and followed the picnickers home. On arrival, he pitched camp in their front garden, spread out his rug and proceeded to eat a hearty supper right there in front of *their* house.

∞

A titled lady living in London found, to her horror, that her boyfriend of six years had secretly taken her great friend away for a dirty weekend. She spent the whole of Sunday sitting outside his front door with a canister of helium. One by one she inflated 1,000 black balloons through his letter box.

When he returned to his home that night, not only did

he have an enormous amount of difficulty opening his door, but could not believe his eyes when confronted with 1,000 black balloons crammed into his rather small mews house.

Looking Good?

'An eye for an eye and a tooth for a tooth.'
Gospel according to St Matthew 5:38

Looking Good?

Rumour has it that there was more to the story than met the eye when President Clinton had his infamous $200 haircut on board Air Force One. During this time the plane sat on the tarmac and the airport was closed for two hours.

Apparently, Hillary always used the services of Christophe of Beverly Hills who had felt horribly snubbed when she had gone to his New York rival for her hairdo for the inaugural celebrations. To get his own back Christophe quite deliberately took ages coiffing the Presidential hair in order to make headlines worldwide and become a household name in the States. He achieved his objective.

∞

Although they had already separated a wife got the full satisfaction of seeing her husband humiliated. While they were still (just) under the same roof, she took his morning suit to some machine embroiderers who emblazoned a magnificent message on his back. He was tipped off at the wedding reception but, too late! Everyone had seen it in church – he had been in the second row. Indeed one man slapped him on the shoulder and asked genially: 'How are you, you little prick?' The message read: '1988 President, Tiny Dicks Club.'

∞

Iain Napier was the perfect house guest but for one problem. The house was a modest affair with just one bathroom for both hosts and guests to share and Iain would insist on using the one and only tooth mug for his false teeth. Everything else was just so perfect in Kenya that everyone tried to overlook it and, after the generator had been switched off in the evening and life reverted to candlelight, it was all so romantic that anything could be forgiven.

The hostess, however, wanted to make a point about the teeth to encourage him to find an alternative site another time. On his final night she made sure that he received their finest hospitality which included copious amounts of alcohol. When he was in bed and well and truly comatose she tiptoed into the bathroom and removed the teeth. Once back in her room she dried them off, took out her bright red nail polish and painted the two front teeth bright red. Once dry she returned them to the contentious mug.

He felt fairly ill in the morning and paid less attention than he should to matters of packing and toilet. He did notice the funny looks he received on the four-hour journey to Nairobi, at check-in and on the aeroplane but it was some time later when he actually went to the loo and caught sight of himself in the mirror.

∞

Two old friends had a major falling out which was sad since they both lived and worked near each other. One had an office in Regent Street, the other ran a major gentleman's clothing store nearby.

Walking back to the office after a good lunch in a fish restaurant one day the businessman developed a severe stomach upset which became more and more critical by the second. Accidents will happen – and did. He rushed, tight-buttocked, into his friend's store to buy a clean pair

of trousers. He was served by the owner himself, who was barely able to disguise his glee at his friend's discomfort and took his time as he wrapped the goods and handed over the carrier bag.

Grabbing the bag our friend limped towards a taxi and ordered it to take him to Liverpool Street Station where he would catch his train home and recover his health in peace. Hardly daring to breathe, he prayed the train would get going quickly. Once it was on the move, he raced to the lavatory. As the train bore him westwards he ripped off his soiled trousers and threw them out of the window. Opening the bag he withdrew his new purchase, only to find that his friend had wrapped him a nice, blue pullover.

∞

A well-known actress understandably asked to remain nameless when relating the revenge she wrought on her lover who had deceived her. Before she walked out she left behind a little souvenir. She tipped black dye in the bottom of his washing machine. His next load was whites only – at least they were before the wash.

∞

Pamella Bordes, spurned lover of ex-*Sunday Times* newspaper editor Andrew Neil, is probably the most famous suit slasher – it was widely reported that she exacted her revenge by cutting the crotch out of each and every one of them.

∞

A dollop of fake tan in a woman's moisturiser can wreak havoc, as discovered by Catherine Small. As the morning progressed people in her office looked at her more and more strangely. It was only when she went to the loo and saw her streaky orange-brown face that she identified

the strange smell that had dogged her all day. Her boyfriend had been increasingly irritated by how much time she spent in front of the mirror and had decided to strike back.

∞

The woman who drenched her erring husband's suits in very nasty cheap perfume had the satisfaction of knowing that they still reeked even after four dry-cleanings . . . and he had to wear one of them to work while the others were being cleaned.

∞

Wimmin's Revenge. There were red shoulders and red faces last May during a scorching London heatwave. On a building site at the corner of Wardour Street and Old Compton Street (aka 'Queer Street'), passing women were greatly amused to see a group of heavily pierced and peroxided young men looking up at the bare-chested builders and in a chorus of cat calls and wolf whistles crying out: 'Hello Boys!' and 'Mmmm, nice buns!'

∞

Perfection can sometimes bring out the absolute worst in people. There was a super-tidy, super-clean lady whose obsessive behaviour inspired her best friend to new heights of school-foolish antics.

Everything in the super-lady's house was immaculate. White was the predominant colour: on sofas, chairs and walls. Everything was arranged just so. Her clothes were perfect, the slightest crease precipitating a change of garment; her hair was always beautifully groomed; she was exactly on time; she never ate or drank too much and bags under the eyes were something she only ever read

about. She was the perfect hostess and dust on the bookshelves just didn't exist in her world. All of this and more drove her friend to distraction so she decided to take action, to rub some of the sheen off the glossy reputation.

Miss Wonderful was having a dinner party (perfection of course) for twenty people when her friend struck. As is often the way, she allowed the ladies to use her bathroom and so, quite soon after her arrival, her best friend needed to 'go'. When she got to the bathroom she withdrew a small pot of Marmite from her bag, found a pair of Miss Wonderful's knickers in the laundry basket and proceeded to spread the Marmite liberally. She left the horrendous looking result hanging half out of the laundry basket before returning to the party. During the course of the evening most of the female guests needed to 'freshen up'. What can they have thought?

∞

A woman well known in the gossip columns became increasingly fed up with her husband. While he was asleep in a drunken stupor she covered him in hair remover. He got up the next morning, had a shower, and all his hair fell off.
– *with thanks to* Daily Express *diarist Ross Benson.*

∞

A new bride was upset when her husband was asked to go shooting in Wales and she was not included in the invitation. His schedule that day was horrific so he asked her if she would pack for him and he would pick up the bag after work and head off west.

On his arrival he was shown to his room and, to his horror, found that the bag contained not shooting gear but white trousers, tennis shoes, a life jacket, thigh-high waders, a Panama hat and his morning suit.

∞

An aristocratic female carefully loosened all the stitching in her husband's suits and shirts. By the time he reached the office he was looking dishevelled. Mid morning, during a meeting, a seam popped lazily open. By lunchtime he was a complete laughing stock and had to go home and change – only to find that she had changed the locks.

Cash Crises

— ∞ —

'Living well is the best revenge.'
        proverb by George Herbert, 1639, and much
favoured by writer and bon viveur Charles Benson

Cash Crises

A woman had been through a fairly unpleasant divorce from her wealthy husband. While they were together they had built up an important collection of china. One particularly fine set comprised twenty-five pieces, of which she had bought eight over the years and he had bought seventeen. He badly wanted them all and he pestered her over and over to let him have them. She simply couldn't decide whether to sell them to him or not.

Tired of the relentless barrage, she eventually summoned an antiques expert. If they were genuine, he told her, they would be worth £2,000 each but, since they were not, they might fetch around £100 each if she were lucky. The decision was easy: she kept absolutely quiet about their being fake and sold her husband the lot for £16,000.

∞

Michael Howard of Leeds changed his name by deed poll to *Yorkshire Bank Plc Are Fascist Bastards* after being charged £20 for a £10 overdraft. The bank has now asked him to close his account and Mr Bastards has asked them to repay the 69p balance by cheque – made out in full in his new name.

∞

A good few years ago a friend of Dorien Manville-Hales became thoroughly fed up with the barrage of letters he received from a high street bank requesting that his £10 or £20 overdraft be settled or his cheques would be bounced. Since he had a fairly good pedigree and his family was clearly not short of money, he was sincerely irked by the pettiness of the bank and its letters. Muttering things about his mother's jewellery, safety and insurance he asked the bank whether he could open a safety deposit box, which was duly granted.

Some time later he walked into the bank and asked to take his box out. He went through all the barriers, procedures and checks, took his box into the windowless room and was left to his own devices. Finally he declared himself finished and the box was put back. Several days later all the people with access to the strong room began to complain about the smell. Shortly afterwards, clients too started to complain: it became worse and worse and really became intolerable. Bank officials investigated the smell and narrowed it down to twelve boxes which, in the circumstances, had to be opened.

Written authority had to be sought from box owners who could be contacted, and the procedure for opening a box without the owner present was a complicated business involving Notaries public and a main board director but at last they managed to get the twelve boxes open.

When they finally discovered which was the offending box the bank wrote to our friend the owner asking why he had put four trout and a camembert into a safety deposit box. His reply was a classic: 'Dear Sirs, Thank you so much for your letter. You have put my mind at rest. I was due to have a dinner party that evening and I have been wondering ever since where I mislaid my shopping.'

∞

Revenge by National Lottery has apparently been perpetrated. Iain Madeley arranged to hold a dinner party one Saturday and invited, among others, a friend who owed him some money and always had a good excuse why he

could not pay it back. This was early in 1995 when the National Lottery was still quite a novelty so, while drinks were being served, Iain handed each guest a lottery ticket for a little fun.

Eight o'clock arrived and the television was switched on amid feverish excitement; even more so when five of the debtor's numbers came up. There were cheers and congratulations, lots of bottles were opened and toasts proposed. With a great flourish he produced his chequebook and generously repaid his debt with interest. Iain hid a smile as he pocketed the cheque: he had played a video recording of the previous week's lottery numbers and had carefully chosen five of the previous week's numbers especially for his friend.

By the time his friend went to claim his winnings, the cheque had been honoured by express clearance.

∞

'When I was in my twenties and still one of the youngest auctioneers in London, I was conducting an auction of nineteenth-century European paintings. Amongst the crowd of gallery owners, collectors and private punters was a German dealer who normally bought cheaper paintings of all schools and styles: English or Spanish, cattle or mothers-with-babies were all meat and drink to him.

'Whenever a painting was selling for less than about £500, a careful glance at him and the auctioneer might catch a twitch, a wink or an almost imperceptible nod of the head; woe betide the auctioneer who missed the bid . . . as I did twice in the first ten lots of the sale.

'On the second miss his deep, guttural and very loud voice boomed out at me: "Vot are you doing young Bonham, are you sleeping or trying to sell pictures?" My response was something to the effect that if he bid more clearly etc., etc.

'The rich, heavily-accented voice broke out again: "Englishman, you are a lousy auctioneer!"

'Now, being told I am a bad auctioneer is as hurtful as being told one is a bad driver or a bad lover (for both of which I have had, thankfully, very few criticisms over the years!). I didn't miss another bid from him; indeed on the twelve lots he bought that auction I pushed him one or two bids higher on each occasion, costing him about £2,000. In 1970 that was a lot of money!

'Ten years later, when he paid me the compliment of being one of the best auctioneers in London, I reminded him of the time, ten years before, when he called me a lousy auctioneer. I also told him it had cost him £2,000. His reaction was slow to come then the loudest laugh I have ever heard burst out. "I vos told to be polite to waiters or they spit into your food. Now I know I haff to add auctioneers to this list!" '
– with thanks to Nick Bonham, deputy chairman, W and F C Bonham and Sons, auctioneers.

∞

A West Country gentleman was fed up with being outbid by dealers in an auction ring. He went to London and bought a splendid collection of rare Japanese Netsuke figures with a view to teaching the ring a lesson.

He put a couple of the items into a local auction in Truro and bought them back himself, paying somewhat over the odds for them, watched all the time by the ring. A few weeks later he did the same, again watched closely by the ring. Then, several weeks later he discovered that the boys were heading up north to a large house sale and he put the rest of his Netsuke figures into it.

The boys in the ring were delighted when they viewed the sale. Yes, they thought, we have a collector back in Truro; he's bound to buy this marvellous collection. They bought the whole lot, at a considerable price owing to a pretty steep reserve. When they were put into auction back in the West Country, no buyer could be found.

∞

Despite receiving written instructions from a customer, a certain local high street bank failed to carry out a request. As a result the customer lost money. A time-consuming argument ensued but the bank would not back down and refused to accept responsibility. Eventually the customer, feeling he was banging his head against a brick wall, told the manager he was fed up and was going to transfer his account to another bank. The manager wrote back in surprised and injured tones, saying that they were 'very sorry that you wish to close the account. Has our service not been to your satisfaction?' The customer wrote back saying: 'Do you realise that an anagram of your bank's name is "Dim and Blank?" '

∞

Probably apocryphal. Robert Maxwell was walking round the office and he saw a man leaning against a wall reading a newspaper.

'How much do you earn?' he asked.

'£150 a week,' came the reply.

Maxwell opened his wallet and pulled out £150 cash. 'Here, take this,' he said. 'You're fired!'

The man took the money and sauntered off. He was not an employee of Maxwell, just a visiting salesman.

∞

Cartoonist and satirist, Alistair Hilleary, otherwise known as 'Loon' was invited to hold an exhibition in the Palace Hotel in St Moritz, a town that has seen its fair share of mayhem and high living. For a diversion one evening, Hilleary and a few others had a little fun 'rearranging' the hotel room of Hamish Leng, another well-known hell-raiser. This caused much mirth but the smile was wiped off Hilleary's face a couple of days later when he was summoned to reception by the management of the Palace who informed him that he was being sought by the Police; his credit rating was nil and would he kindly explain himself or they would have no alternative but to turn him, and his seventy-two paintings, on to the streets. Hilleary was made to sweat good and proper: the Swiss took a very dim view of the situation. It was hours later when he caught sight of the fax from the Acme Credit Control Agency in England . . . and recognised its address as that of one Mr Leng.

Military Mischief

— ∞ —

'Always forgive your enemies – but never forget
their names.'

Robert Kennedy

Military Mischief

An extremely arrogant young French cavalry officer from a very aristocratic background arrived at the officers' mess of a British regiment. It was pretty quickly assessed that he was going to be a difficult one. He was standoffish and, despite several attempts to include him and make him feel welcome, he did not let up and upset everyone he came into contact with. One night over dinner he informed the assembled company of officers in the mess that, as far as he was concerned, the French army was vastly superior in terms of ability and style to their British counterparts. A red rag to a bull.

As a result it was decided by several of the younger members of the officers' mess that he needed to be taught a lesson, and the more stylish a lesson the better. One night over dinner it was explained to him that a couple of members of the mess had found an extremely convenient and highly illegal route into what was then East Germany and that they would be taking a party of officers across that night to go and party hard in an East German pub where women and beer flowed all night. It was, of course, an extremely hazardous operation so only the bravest and most outstanding officers would go – would he be interested in joining them? His Gallic pride could not resist this temptation. He agreed. It is worth noting at this point that the regiment's location was some distance from the East German border but it was located close to a major range complex which was sealed

119

off by barbed wire fences and manned checkpoints which, to the uninitiated, did look like border crossing points.

The French officer and three British officers set off in one of the subaltern's cars and proceeded to spend about an hour driving around in a large circle using several different autobahns, giving the impression that they were, in fact, travelling to the inner German border. They arrived at the entry point to one of the ranges where, waiting for them, were two young officers dressed in Russian uniforms and carrying Russian replica machine-guns which they had borrowed from the regiment's training wing. At the checkpoint one of the officers in the car expressed some concern that it was highly unusual to have Russians on the gate and that the normal border guard who let them through did not seem to be there. He gave the Frenchman the customary bottle of whisky used for bribing the guards on such occasions and told him to get out and give it to them.

As he approached, one of the 'Russians' stepped forward and addressed him in fluent Czechoslovak – a language unknown to the young Frenchman. After five minutes of torrential Czech abuse the Frenchman offered the bottle which was promptly smashed by the bogus guard who then, at machine-gunpoint, marched him into a dark corner where his hands were tied and a hood put over his head. He was told he was under arrest and would be taken to KGB HQ for interrogation.

The Frenchman was thrown into the back of a 'military vehicle' and driven for another long period round in circles until they arrived at the officers' mess where he was manhandled into the cellars and tied to a chair in front of a table on which there was a strong reading light pointing at him so that when the hood was removed, he could see nothing. He assumed he was alone. He cowered – not knowing twenty officers had crammed in to watch the proceedings.

The Orderly Officer appeared. In his hands he carried a silver tray on which was a bottle of champagne and a glass and the Frenchman was asked politely whether he would care to drink the health of his host regiment. It took several hours to convince the terrified young man that he wasn't actually in East Germany.

After a considerable amount of pride-swallowing and a rather spurious excuse about a sick relation, he was never seen again.

∞

A member of the Welsh Guards recalls a time when, on exercise in Germany, they were allocated a cook from the Army Catering Corps. He was a large man and, amongst other irritating habits, he simply would not use the latrines. Every morning he would go into the bushes outside the perimeter fence to perform his evacuations. One morning the boys decided to follow him – he was not a tactical man and did not notice them behind him in the bracken. They watched him as he held on to a branch and squatted. Gently they slipped a long-handled shovel underneath him. The cook deposited his load right in the middle and the boys quietly removed it. They could hardly restrain their giggles as they saw the corpulent corporal turn to inspect his deposit and see – nothing! Puzzlement registered in his expression and, ashen-faced, he returned to base. It was evidently a sobering experience as he returned to the spot later and was seen scrabbling through the leaves, still seeking the evidence.

∞

Sir Reginald Bennett tells us of a young officer in an RAF mess who made a thorough nuisance of himself – he would regularly become drunk and rude, and then would become violent and start breaking things, and would

usually end each binge by throwing up. Everyone was fed up with him and warned him that if he went on doing this he would sick up his own guts. This had absolutely no effect on him – he continued to drink too much. The others decided that this had to stop and enough was enough.

One day, during one of his binges, they got hold of some rabbits' entrails and waited until he reeled off to bed. When he was safely asleep they crept into his room and put them all over his pillow and face. The next day he was supposed to be on duty and he appeared at breakfast, white as a sheet, very cowed and quite unlike his usual bumptious self. When asked if something was wrong he replied: 'As a matter of fact something rather awful happened. You remember you warned me more than once that if I continued to drink an awful lot and get sick that one day I would throw up my own guts? I'm sorry to say it actually happened last night – but I managed to get them back down again.'

∞

A tidy act of military revenge took place during the Second World War. The Pioneer Corps regiment did a lot of the less popular jobs in the Army: digging latrines, building huts and being really resourceful at obtaining and replacing broken items and parts. During the march through Normandy and Belgium a few of them were billeted at a farmhouse. The farmer's wife was an old harridan who, they said, milked the system and wanted all the perks. When the army was to move on they offered to do some decorating in her house. She was delighted and they worked like mad. One of the rooms they did was her loo which they left in pristine condition – they even redecorated her toilet seat! She only found out later that they had used varnish that never dried.

– *with thanks to Christopher Rhys-Jones.*

∞

Squadron Leader Peter Tomlinson, ADC to 'Bomber' Harris and brother of Mary Poppins' star David Tomlinson, was a prisoner of war in Stalag 3, the Royal Air Force Officers' POW camp, for four years. It was practice for prisoners to pool their Red Cross parcels and for an unfortunate volunteer to do the most creative cooking and preparation that was possible in the circumstances. Standard additional rations were a few potatoes, some bread and half a horse to make into a soup. One particular volunteer only took on the job with great reluctance and on the strict condition that no one was ever to complain or he would give up. He was hoist by his own petard when everyone made a supreme effort not to complain and he found himself still doing the cooking three months later.

He decided to get his own back and invite criticism: when he was collecting the rations from the horse-drawn cart he picked up some balls of horse manure as well. He rolled the balls in bread crumbs, fried them and served them up to the unsuspecting prisoners. One of them took a mouthful and exclaimed: 'Oh my God, horse shit!' Realising that this might lose them their cook he quickly added: '. . . but bloody well cooked!'

∞

Col Peter Rogers of The Blues and Royals is the Lieutenant Colonel Commanding Household Cavalry and 'Silver Stick in Waiting'. He is very good looking and charming and, back in his day, was one of London's more popular Debs' Delights. In the early Seventies he was stationed at Knightsbridge with the Household Cavalry Mounted Regiment and was asked to make up a party of people going to one of the most popular shows in the West End at the time. However, he admits

he was a little naughty – at the last moment he had a hot date and he stood his friends up. They were not best pleased.

A few months later Rogers received a very smart invitation from Lady Paget for her daughter: At Home, Quaglinos, Dinner and Dancing; Dress: White Tie. Rogers thought this a little odd as he didn't know a Lady Paget so he looked through the books and found a Lady Paget in Somerset. He telephoned her, to ask whether she was giving a party for her daughter. 'Not as far as I know,' she replied tartly. He also thought white tie (i.e. full evening dress) was improbable. His concern was slightly eased by the fact that Lady Paget's invitation was appearing on brother officers' mantelpieces – Richard Wilkinson, John Greenaway (now Sir John) and Dick Morrisey-Paine were also going and there was a certain safety in numbers. He was still mystified even while changing for the party on the evening and, to reassure himself, he went along to Charles Horsfall's room, but he had already left for the party. 'No problem,' he thought as he set off in a taxi to Quaglinos and was met in the foyer by a waiter who inquired: 'Lady Paget's party? Please follow me.' Rogers peered through the door and saw the band in full swing. As he pitched in and found himself by the dance floor, he realised that everyone else was in *black* tie (far less formal). By then he was on the stage in full view of the assembled company. The band instantly struck up and everyone who wasn't laughing too much sang along: 'I'm putting on my top hat, doing up my *white tie* . . .' It was all taken in good grace and the boys offered to buy him dinner. Rogers chose all the most expensive things on the menu.

∞

'In 1953, while doing my National Service as a Second Lieutenant in the 10th Royal Hussars, I was on a "Survival

Course" in Germany with my troop of three Centurion tanks. Survival in this case meant living off the land for two weeks without rations or cash.

'We camped in a forest which turned out to belong to a most gentle and generous German aristocrat. I knew this to be so because one evening he invited me to dine with him in his castle. In order to treat the occasion with proper respect I donned my officer's uniform and arrived at the castle gates at 7 p.m. Imagine my surprise when I found that a Signal Corps Brigadier had also been invited for the same reason. He had bivouacked a whole brigade within the generous confines of the estate.

The three of us sat down to a gargantuan feast in an enormous dining hall. Course after course was washed down with continuous libations. The Brigadier was quite unable to cope with this generosity and soon began to insult both our host and me. He made a number of insulting toasts to the Germans in general and our host in particular, but soon, concentrating on the one least able to defend himself, he turned his attention to me. He patently disliked me intensely. He disliked the Armoured Corps, cavalry regiments, toffee-nosed subalterns and, for what seemed an eternity, I was subjected to a torrent of abuse – all because I was a junior officer to the Brigadier.

'Coming to the end of his tirade he challenged me to find and attack his brigade before daylight. Very quietly our host inquired whether this was an order, and the Brigadier confirmed that it was just that. As he was driven off in a drunken stupor, our host came round the castle in an old Bugatti and offered me a lift. His purpose soon became clear when I realised that he was following the Brigadier back to his camp without lights so that I could discover the whereabouts of his brigade. They were in a small wood nearby. All the vehicles were under camouflage netting and there was no sentry on duty. As the Brigadier tumbled into his tent, my host and I returned to my troop. Twelve rather sleepy men started up the tanks and we retraced our tracks to the Brigadier. We surrounded the camp with a trail of diesel oil and, as we drove away, we were confident that the whole brigade was on fire.

'The sweetest part of the revenge was not so much the conflagration, but the hand-written note from the German which awaited me upon my return to camp. It read: "In the event of your court martial, I would be honoured to attend on your behalf to confirm that you were obeying an order to a *junior officer*." '
– *with thanks to Anthony Snow, the well-respected chairman of Hill and Knowlton (UK) Ltd.*

∞

A trouper in the Queen's Royal Irish Hussars was on exercise in Germany – his specific duty was to look after the officers' mess tent which was a marvellous affair, equipped for great comfort with furniture and paintings. The officers' latrines were in a tent behind the mess tent, behind which was another tent and the soldiers' latrine was beyond that. Trouper North got into the habit of using the officers' latrines rather than the soldiers'. He also smoked like a chimney and more than once Major Christopher Hanbury warned him that he should not smoke in the latrines, with a merry caution that 'it's neat alcohol down there!' Trouper North still did not desist, however, so between them, a few officers hatched a plot to stop him by pouring petrol down their latrine. Later, they saw North creep in and, a few minutes later, there was an almighty explosion and North was expelled, airborne, followed by a torrent of the latrines' contents. There was, apparently, little hair left on his body. He dutifully made the long journey to the soldiers' latrines in future.

∞

It was common practice among officers in a certain regiment to get their own back on someone by placing a small pebble in the back left hubcap of their car. This would produce a little rattle which, because it was on the far side of the car from the driver, would be almost impossible to trace and would even baffle the garage mechanics to whom the cars were sent.

Animal Antics

— ∞ —

'People who fight fire with fire usually end up
with ashes.'
  'Dear Abby' newspaper column, 7 March 1974

Animal Antics

'Tiny' is the name of the large stuffed shark which hung in the Food Halls of Harrods for some time as part of the continuing feud between Tiny Rowland and Mohammed Al Fayed. Here Mr Al Fayed, chairman of Harrods, explains the true story of events.

'When Mr Leo Kennedy, a London shipping broker, caught a record-breaking Mako shark off Mauritius something inspired him to telephone me from his holiday hotel offering me the beast. I accepted immediately and arranged for the shark to be placed in the care of a skilled taxidermist and shipped to me at Brompton Road. I knew that, whatever had happened to him in his life, the shark's true destiny now lay ahead of him.

Checking only to make sure that there was a good likeness, I ordered Tiny to be taken to the Food Halls and suspended over the smoked salmon counter, his new name proudly painted upon the dorsal fin.

His arrival was widely reported and Tiny soon became a must-see on the list of London attractions. As Mr Tiny Rowland's vendetta ran out of steam and it was clear to everyone that there was no justice to it, so his demands for recompense grew more ambitious. I ignored them. I said, and often repeated, that the only concessions I would ever make were as follows – I would shake Mr Rowland's hand, I would give him a

jolly good lunch and I would take down his fishy namesake from his place of honour. And so it came to pass that on 22 October 1993, Mr Rowland and I signed a one-page peace agreement thus ending his fifteen-year quest for Harrods. We then proceeded in a spirit of good fellowship to the Food Halls where together we winched down Tiny to general applause and the clatter of the Nikon choir.

By this time Tiny had acquired a small shark in his formidable jaws, the small shark bearing the name Bock in honour of Mr Rowland's new partner and then co-chief executive Herr Dieter Bock. As the journalist reviewing the newspapers on the following morning's broadcast of radio's *Today* programme remarked: 'It is not often that the fish counter at Harrods makes the front page of every broadsheet newspaper.' Later Mr Rowland and I enjoyed several convivial lunches together.

As for Tiny, I took him by Harrods horse-drawn delivery van to Mr Rowland's house in Chester Square. Mr Rowland had planned to hang Tiny over his swimming pool but he magnanimously agreed to my suggestion that the shark perform one final public service. Tiny was auctioned by Sotheby's – who generously waived their fee – for £4,000; the money going to the excellent charity ChildLine. Tiny is now the star attraction at a marine world theme park in Scotland.'

∞

There was to be a dinner party in a rather grand old house in Southern Ireland. The food was all prepared and the guests arrived. The hostess went into the kitchen to sort out the canapés and was horrified to see the family cat nibbling the beautifully-displayed salmon. She gave the cat an enormous belt which launched it half-way across the room and tidied up the fish, covering the bits

that the cat had eaten with cucumber and lemon and generally patting it back into shape.

The evening proceeded well. After the main course, however, the hostess was even more horrified to find the cat in the kitchen again but, this time, lying on the floor stone cold dead. She immediately thought of the salmon and her guests and was overwhelmed with fear for their safety. Quickly she telephoned her doctor who prescribed radical treatment immediately. Each and every one of her guests went to the casualty department to have their stomachs pumped.

Some time afterwards the results of the autopsy on the cat were returned. The cat had its ultimate revenge – it had actually died of a heart attack.

∞

'This happened while I was an apprentice rider. One of the lads had been getting a lot more rides, and was really condescending about the way I rode. He just wasn't very pleasant over quite a period of time. While he was working in another yard he was down to ride a horse which had a good chance of winning in a Conditional Jockeys' Race (a "boys" race). I got one of the lads in my yard to phone the trainer's secretary and say that his horse was not running as it had gone lame. So he didn't show up. But I did. I went on to win. I haven't really looked back since.'
– *John Francome, jockey and TV presenter.*

∞

The crew of a racing boat became progressively more and more irritated by the rich owner of a large dog. He would let it off his gin palace on to the dock where it would roam around all day, getting in everyone's way and, more often than not, doing its doings in places where it would inevitably end up on a sail or a sailor. They tried

to get it to stay out of their way by kicking it into the water from time to time, where it would flounder around like Scooby Doo for a while, but always it returned to haunt them.

When they could take no more they devised a simple revenge – the big, hungry dog was more than delighted to eat the sump oil sandwiches which they fed it just before it was due back on the gin palace.

Sump oil has the same effect on the digestion as castor oil and they had a good laugh imagining the state of the smart carpets in the motor yacht.

∞

'I had been out deep-sea fishing for the day and had been lucky enough to land a big barracuda. This, I thought, could provide us with a little amusement that night. We decided to slip it under Ralph Glister's pillow and scare the pants off him when he turned in, particularly as his wife Kathie was in on the joke and had in fact told us that Gillie always slept with his arms stretched out under his head. The fearsome-looking fish was duly placed in his bed and the rest of the family and myself gathered quietly in the ante-room of the Glisters' suite to hear what happened.

'We heard Gillie say good-night to Kathie. He yawned, then slid between the sheets. Don Miles nearly burst a rib trying to keep quiet during the next half-minute of silence which was then broken by a howl from the other side of the door.

' "Jesus Christ!" came Gillie's voice. "Kathy! What the hell . . ." By this time he was out of bed and the lights went on in the room. Gillie was last seen rushing out of the other bedroom door yelling. "Chief, chief," he hollered. "Where are you, you . . ."

'The sight of him dashing down the hotel corridor, where we presently found him, was worth a million

139

dollars. Gillie, we noticed, wore a red flannel nightshirt down to his ankles and with this thing flapping about and a damned great fish in his arms, he looked like an escapee from a nuthouse. We even got the house detective on the phone, telling him that there was a madman on the penthouse floor rushing about in a red nightshirt with a barracuda in his hand. Poor Glister was nearly locked up – and he didn't think it too hilariously funny at the time, either!'
– *from* All Arms and Elbows, *the autobiography of high-spirited racing driver, the late Innes Ireland.*

∞

A man who lived at a smart Chelsea address became thoroughly fed up with a dog-owner who constantly allowed his pet to foul the footway right in front of his house. Over and over again he would set off for work and step right in it.

Eventually he decided enough was enough so he kept vigil from early one morning until the culprits, as usual, stopped right outside his house and the dog did its business. Instead of confronting them he quietly followed them back to their home and noted their address.

Later, when the urge hit him, he collected a large offering of his own and wrapped it in newspaper. He went to the dog-owner's house and put it, newspaper and all, on his front doorstep. Quickly he set fire to the paper, rang the doorbell and ran away to the safety of a pillar on the other side of the street. He was able to watch the horrified dog owner jump all over the burning package, thus spreading its contents all over his shoes and the doormat.

∞

Sweet Revenge

In the front of a lovely shop in Castle Street, Cirencester, they sold butterflies of every colour, shape and description. In the back was a shop selling reptiles, dangerous insects and spiders. It offered a mail-order service but eventually had to close as so many people were using the service to send nasty animals to their unsuspecting enemies.

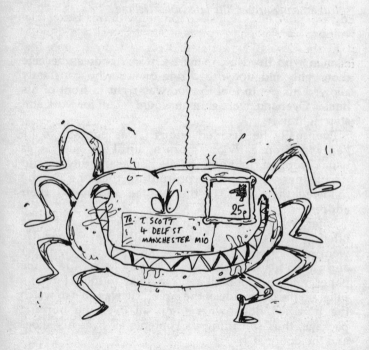

∞

When Edward and Lizzie Hughes invited their friends the Stevens for the weekend they didn't consider the implications when they asked whether they could bring their dog. 'Sure,' they said, but soon regretted their bonhomie.

On arrival the big, floppy Bassett hound jumped up and laddered Lizzie's tights, it went around hoovering the food (including all the snacks and some of their supper) and proceeded to howl endlessly. Enough, thought Edward, none of us will sleep tonight with this racket. He wrapped a Mogadon in a piece of leftover steak and slipped it to the dog. Peace reigned. It wasn't until noon the following day that they found the dog. It was fast asleep and snoring blissfully in the herbaceous border.

∞

Keif was a beagley-mongrel who belonged to Jane Stonborough's family when she was little. He was the most intelligent and dignified dog, and he was responsible for the only case of genuine canine revenge we have encountered.

Jane's cousin Derish came over to their house one day and, after lunch, lit a huge cigar. Derish delighted in tormenting Keif – over and over again he would take a huge puff and blow it right into the face of Keif, who responded with great dignity for a while. Finally Keif could take it no more and walked away . . . to Derish's bedroom. Jumping on to the table, he took the other cigar in his mouth and returned to the drawing room. He then walked up to where Derish was sitting, broke the cigar into pieces and dropped it at Derish's feet, whereupon he sat down and stared at the man in a manner that can only be interpreted as contempt.

∞

'It was, for me at least, love at first sight,' said Jane Capp about her boyfriend Tom. Tom swept her off her feet with flowers and romantic weekends in the country. 'We really hit it off both in and out of bed,' she added, 'I thought I'd met the man of my dreams.'

She hadn't. Tom was spotted canoodling with a mystery girl by a friend of Jane's. When Jane confronted Tom his attitude was 'what you don't know can't hurt you'. 'But I did know and it did hurt me,' said Jane. 'I wanted to buy him something that would tell him exactly how I felt.'

With this thought in mind she went to a pet shop, bought a dead white rat, attached a tag to its leg saying 'Tom' and then she posted it to him. 'I think he got the message,' said Jane.

∞

A naughty stable owner disguised a winning horse with boot polish and entered it into a novice race. Naturally it won, bringing substantial gains to the owner and trainer.

'Quick!' said the owner to one of the lads, 'get rid of the horse!'

Unfortunately, he took the owner literally. Several days later the owner asked to see the horse and the lad said proudly: 'Don't worry, I shot it and put it down a mine shaft.'

∞

When Ernie Perkins bought an old gravel pit and started commercial tipping, his neighbours began to complain. It all came to a head when Gloucestershire County Council ordered Mr Perkins to cease operations, even

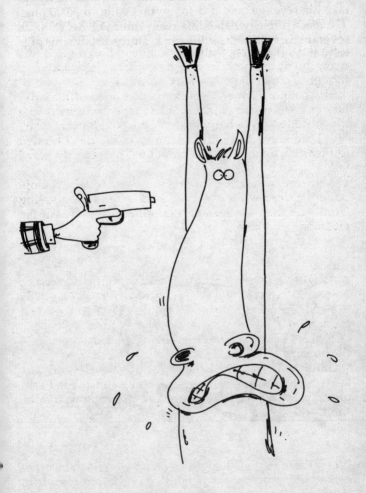

though the pit was not full. He announced that he would take his revenge, and did so, by investing in 3,000 pigs. 'I'll teach them what stink really means,' he said, as several score prime, swill-eating, slurry-producing pigs were unloaded on to his land.

∞

'After three happy years he suddenly behaved monstrously, during December. In order to leave it all behind and get on with my life revenge was important.

He is an artistic man, obsessive and prone to panic reactions. He is also an expert plantsman and has a beautiful garden alongside a side street, with a 4'6" fence. Slugs send him into paroxysms of rage. I waited until May when the plants were up, growing and juicy, by which time I had devised a fitting act of vengeance. With the help of a friend we leafleted all the surrounding streets with the following notice:

NON TOXIC SLUG CONTROL RESEARCH PROJECT

DO YOU HATE KILLING SLUGS?

Natural scientific research welcomes your healthy,
unwanted slugs.
Please place them in our research garden centre at:

5, GEORGE STREET,
CHICHESTER

Easy access and parking

Research results will be published in the
November edition of Green Magazine.

'Mud- and rain-smudged notes were put through his letter box with information about where the slugs had been placed. Ladies with flowing hands wrote from afar, one thus: "I have put 36 slugs in your left-hand border.

Such a pretty garden. Are you sure you are doing the right thing?" He has no idea how many slugs he was given. I felt much better."

∞

A jilted banker had a poster made up and photocopied with his unfaithful girlfriend's picture, bearing the caption 'Have you seen this Dog?' He nailed it on to trees all over west London.

Telephone Trouble

— ∞ —

'Sweet is revenge – especially to women.'
Lord Byron, 1788–1824

Telephone Trouble

A woman scorned worked out that the way really to upset her control-freak former lover was through his address book. She carefully changed all the telephone numbers, postcodes and street numbers around. The threes became eights, the ones became fours and Cs became Os.
– with thanks to Royal correspondent Ingrid Seward.

∞

Several years ago, TV personality Sarah Greene returned home from a couple of days' filming to find fifty-six messages on her telephone answering machine. When she played them back they were all from the same person who had obviously heard her husband, presenter Mike Smith, on the answerphone tape and thought it was a terrific wheeze to hear it over and over again.

As she listened through the messages, keen to hear whether any of their friends or colleagues had been able to get through, it became clear that her mystery caller worked near a company's switchboard. She could hear people answering telephones with: 'Good Morning, Superglaze,' in the background.

Sarah looked them up in the phone book and discovered they were a large glazing and double-glazing company. A simple complaint to the management for timewasting and blocking their answerphone tape didn't seem like much fun and Sarah and Mike felt like a little light revenge.

Sarah put on her best plummy voice and asked to speak to the chairman or managing director. She introduced herself as Jane Tompkinson, PA to the chairman of British Telecom. Could she, she asked, arrange a high level meeting to discuss a large contract that they were putting out to tender? She could hear the growing excitement amongst the staff and the general manager was fawning and ingratiating as he asked whether 'Jane' could divulge the nature of the contract. 'Jane' replied that at this stage it was highly confidential but was he familiar with the Telecom Tower? Sarah could almost hear the champagne corks popping.

After a suitable interval Mike and Sarah came clean to the now bitterly disappointed general manager and left *him* to deal with Mike's ardent fan.

∞

A well-known re-insurance broker, tired of his girlfriend's infidelity, had call-cards made up bearing her telephone number and a voluptuous description of her. Then he put them in twenty telephone boxes in and around Soho.

∞

Derek Nimmo was invited to host a 24-hour charity telethon in Auckland, New Zealand. Having flown there at his own expense, he was particularly dismayed to be greeted at his hotel by a somewhat hostile Barry Christiansen, Collector of Taxes, who, in a most uncharitable manner, was demanding an outstanding payment dating back over five years. Feeling extremely jet-lagged and more than a little nervous about the forthcoming marathon programme, he asked if Mr Christiansen would mind contacting him the following day. This was not to be. Mr Christiansen dogged him at every turn, eventually popping up at the TV studio.

Enough was enough – Derek Nimmo, before going on air, looked up Barry Christiansen's name in the telephone directory and, as the many pledges were coming in, announced that a most charming man by the name of Barry Christiansen at the following telephone number had promised that, for every person who telephoned him within the next six hours, he would donate $20 to the cause.

∞

When she found out her boyfriend was being unfaithful, a certain lady let herself into his flat one Friday and dialled the speaking clock . . . in New York. One can only imagine his face when he returned on the Sunday, found the telephone off the hook, picked it up and worked out why the time and the accent were wrong.

∞

Morocco is a country where the wealthiest families live in stunning, interior-designed homes, think nothing of nipping to Paris for a little gentle shopping, and the women are sweet to each other – until their backs are turned.

One of these beautifully-groomed ladies needed to get her own back on another. She telephoned her, putting on her best Italian accent and said that she was from Italian *Vogue* and wanted to send a photographer and writer to do a feature on her house, garden and friends. Would she please have a ladies' lunch party which would be photographed for the feature? The date was agreed.

Anticipation of the event was feverish: ten women working out what to wear, how to have their hair done, when to arrive . . . and the hostess went wild, having the house spring cleaned, ordering imported fresh flowers and the finest foods: the best of everything that money could buy.

The great day came, the women assembled in a cloud

of perfume and designer clothes. The hostess became a little uneasy as time marched on and the *Vogue* team had not shown up, but she was greatly reassured when the telephone rang and the Italian voice assured them that the team was on its way but *do* start lunch.

History doesn't relate when the penny finally dropped nor the humiliation suffered by the hostess.

∞

Many years ago in a lovely house overlooking the Hamble River, a man became aware that his pretty wife was, once again, involved in a long and lovey-dovey telephone conversation with her lover. Time to act, he thought as he grabbed his car keys.

He knew that his adversary would be in the telephone box on the village green so he drove slowly to the box and reversed up against the door so that it could not be opened. With that he got out, locked the car and disappeared for the day.

∞

Corinna Liddell was amongst a party of beautiful people at Tramp. She was with her boyfriend but this did not stop another member of the party from flirting with her all the time and, whenever her boyfriend went off to the loo or to dance with someone, he would home in on her and pester her for her telephone number. Gilbert badgered her over and over and just would not give up so, finally, she leaned towards him, rested her chin on her hand, looked into his eyes and oh, so sweetly recited a telephone number.

It made her laugh every time she imagined him trying to call her. She had given him the telephone number of an extremely graphic recorded message outlining the causes, symptoms and medical procedures for venereal diseases.

Culinary Capers

— ∞ —

'Revenge – a dish that should be eaten cold.'
King Victor Emmanuel II of Italy, 1787

Culinary Capers

Nowadays, if you order a pizza from a pizzeria which delivers, they insist on taking your telephone number and, usually, call you back to confirm. However, before they got wise to it, it was possible to order a pizza to be delivered to an address without the recipient ever knowing who was responsible. A very respectable American lady tells of how strangely ungracious her ex-boyfriend was to receive and have to pay for a huge pizza (with extra peppers and anchovies) at 2 a.m. when he was in the throes of passion with his new girlfriend.

∞

According to Dee Knight, her husband John was unbelievably mean with the housekeeping and wouldn't even give her money for food. Dee sold her jewellery to buy food for them and her daughter but even then John complained about the cooking. When he walked out after thirteen months of marriage Dee took her revenge before she moved to her new flat.

First stop was the local cash and carry where she spent £300. Then to the local fish shops followed by visits to all the shops that sold paddling pools in St Brelade, Jersey. Then she returned to the marital home and prepared a three-course meal that her soon-to-be ex-husband would not forget.

She blew up the fifteen pools and placed them around the house. In the spare room she filled one with three

161

hundred cans of chicken soup. Another in the couple's bedroom she filled with twenty-four rotting prawns and fifty stinking fish heads. On the landing another contained festering fish guts topped up with tinned tomatoes. She filled up two pools in the sitting room with 180 pounds of mashed potato and a further four she filled with gravy. Other pools contained two dozen apples, with a gallon of custard and another contained 1,322 stewing tea-bags.

It took Dee a week to prepare and the one thing she was unhappy with was the custard: 'Because it has lumps in it, but I just hope one goes down the wrong way.' Dee added, 'By the time he finds the mess the stench will be unbearable. The beauty of using paddling pools is that once they are full they are impossible to move without everything slopping out, and if they start to deflate there will be an even bigger mess!'

∞

An aristocratic landowner was tired of providing endless hospitality every weekend for the same bunch of ungrateful 'friends' and decided it was time to get his own back. He telephoned them all and asked them to come and stay, and received a chorus of 'Oh rather!' and 'Goody!' They all showed up on the Friday night.

After dinner on the Saturday night: a delicious repast with plenty of champagne and fine claret, their host proposed that they play a game. 'Splendid!', 'Absolutely marvellous, good show!' brayed the assembled company. Their host informed them that he had bought a number of goodies from Asprey and there would be prizes for everyone: it was a sort of a treasure hunt and, just to make it a little different and more exciting, why didn't they all have their ankles shackled together so that everyone could find the prize at the same time? What a riot, they all agreed and they were duly shackled by the butler.

What they had not been told was that the cook had prepared two quite separate meals, one for the host and another for the guests – the latter having been liberally laced with laxative. Our host had the most entertaining evening as the stricken guests alternately had to dive into bushes, pulling with them the rest of the guests to witness their discomfort.

∞

Every time she discovered that her husband had been cheating on her, a woman made him a curry – with tinned dog meat. 'He hadn't a clue and I still chuckle when I think of him tucking in. I would tell him he was my PAL, or a real CHUM, as he chomped on the doggy dinner.'

∞

Eminent violinist and musician Jack Rothstein, who is a great wit and raconteur, tells of the musicians in Billy Cotton's band who used to tour the country. To save on costs they would stay in bed-and-breakfast accommodation for around £3.10s a week, which included a light meal in the evening after the show.

They were staying near Liverpool and two of them who were sharing a room decided that a bottle of sherry would brighten up the landlady's standard offering of corned beef salad, trifle and tea, so they duly bought a bottle and had a couple of drinks each. The following evening, they took out their bottle and thought that the level seemed to have dropped – so they put a marker on it to see if someone else was drinking it. Sure enough, the next evening the level was well below their mark.

They decided to put a stop to this by finishing the bottle and replacing the contents with their own pee. The next night, they were horrified to see that the level had fallen again and on the final night a great deal went

missing. They did, however, have a jolly good laugh trying to envisage their victim and the effect that their beverage would be having on him or her.

As they were settling up with the landlady, she asked whether they had had a nice time.

'Yes,' they replied, 'but you had better be careful. We think you might have a thief here.'

'How so?' she asked, much agitated and they explained about the falling sherry level.

'Oh,' she smiled, 'don't worry about it. It was me. I was only using it to make your trifle.'

∞

Jojo Leatham was angry. Her husband Mark had had far too much brandy at a dinner party the night before and she felt he deserved every bit of his evil hangover. She had heard him crash around the room at 4 a.m. rattling the last of the Nurofen and madly trying to rehydrate. The following morning she was in the kitchen and one of the children was sent down to 'ask Mummy for something for my headache.' He innocently swallowed the two sleeping pills she sent up to him. They had a large lunch party that day and he couldn't understand why his head kept falling in the soup.

∞

We are told that American TV chat show host Tom Snyder was interviewing a lovely young actress on his show some years ago. It was fairly obvious that his interest in her was more than just professional and she, consequently, became very uncomfortable. Nevertheless, when he invited her out to dinner a couple of days later she accepted with great pleasure and suggested an unbelievably expensive restaurant that she would like to try. He duly booked a table but she, apparently, telephoned the restaurant and changed the reservation to a table for

twelve and invited ten of her friends. It is much to his credit that he had the good grace to pay for them all.

∞

Kerry Packer had had a long day playing polo at Windsor and it is rumoured that he, along with a party of ten players and others arrived back at Midhurst, tired and hungry. It was about ten o'clock at night and Packer wanted to buy supper for the group so they found a restaurant whose lights were on and went in. They were refused a table: the kitchens were closing, sorry, they'd have to go somewhere else. They went along to a second establishment where the request was similarly greeted with refusal. The proprietress of the third restaurant was unwilling at first to serve a large party when everyone else was just leaving but eventually agreed, saying that they could rustle up some steak and chips – she'd just go and get her husband out of bed.

After a delicious supper and a few bottles of wine, Kerry Packer asked for the bill which was duly presented. He allegedly handed over a cheque for £10,000, which was conditional on their showing it to the owners of the two other restaurants which had turned him down. A number of restaurants in and around Midhurst have since put up signs saying: 'Kerry Packer Welcome Here'.

∞

Phillip Seldon was the founding editor of *Vintage* magazine and published it for seventeen years. Self-publicist, Marvin Shanken, publishes rival magazine *Wine Spectator*. Shanken booked a table at the very expensive Bouley restaurant in New York City and wrote a report of his meal in *Wine Spectator* trashing the restaurant, criticising it for keeping him waiting for his table and for poor service.

A piece about his report subsequently appeared in the gossip column of the *New York Post*, one of New York's biggest papers, and Phillip Seldon decided to act. He sent a letter to the letters page of the *New York Post*, saying how a restaurant needs more than good food to be successful; it needs ambience and beautiful people. It went on to say that Marvin Shanken is fat and ugly and deserved to be mistreated. The *New York Post* printed the letter.

∞

Dai Llewellyn was very proud of his brand new Lancia. It was parked, all gleaming and new, outside a well-known restaurant while he and a few friends had dinner. They were the last to leave and, on returning to the car, found a dozen bin bags full of restaurant rubbish piled against it. Mr Llewellyn asked the waiters to move them and they refused. A heated argument followed, during which the rubbish was emptied into the car. Dai's old Harrovian friend sloped off, complaining of a bad back, leaving Dai and two girls to sort matters out with six, burly waiters. Fighting broke out and, eventually, Dai, battered and bruised, conceded the unequal struggle. He decided to get his own back and hit them in the pocket where it hurt.

Over the next few weeks he completely booked the restaurant out several times with false bookings, taking enormous pleasure in adopting different accents, making elaborate bookings for fictitious peers of the realm; taking tables for business functions; booking a party of twelve for his wife's birthday (complete with personalised cake); ordering special menus for overseas visitors; making bookings with intricate details and additions. He would only stop when the restaurant refused a booking saying: 'Sorry, Sir, there are no tables available: we are completely full tonight.'

Surprisingly, the restaurant is still going twenty years on, and both parties are the best of friends.

∞

'I was very interested in a famous and very powerful man but, stupidly, went and introduced him to a well-known widow. Mistake. The next thing I knew they had arranged lunch together at Mosimans. I know the people there very well and worked out the couple's timings – they would be arriving at one-ish, have an aperitif, and by around 1.45 p.m. they would be mellow and relaxed . . .

I arranged for a single white rose to be delivered at that time, with a note that read: "Why play the fiddle when you can have a Stradivarius?" A couple of friends were positioned in the restaurant at tables nearby to witness the scene and testified that her face fell a mile and he went bright red. It achieved its objective: she never talked to me again. But he did. Definitely!'
– *with many thanks to writer Mona Bauwens.*

∞

'A new and dazzling Soho brasserie opened in the early Eighties and a friend of mine suggested we eat there. So it was that, one hot summer's day, we found ourselves sitting by the window enjoying a pre-prandial drink, waiting for a roast beef salad. It duly arrived, looking very beautiful with its fashionable, designer leaves and, without further ado, we dug in. Simon speared a tomato and was just about to pop it in his mouth when he stopped and turned deathly pale. He was trembling – I truly thought he was having a heart attack. Indicating his plate he revealed the source of his pallor: a huge black spider was residing in his lunch. It turned my stomach too – you don't expect to find arachnids in your entrées.

'As the seconds passed I began to have doubts – it

really was improbably large. Closer scrutiny revealed that it was, in fact, plastic. We called the restaurant manager and asked him to explain matters and he assumed it was our little joke. We assured him that we had not put it there ourselves – and how could we possibly fake the colour of poor Simon's face? He disappeared to investigate.

'A quarter of an hour later he reappeared with a trembling sous-chef who admitted the whole thing. He had chosen the recipient at random. The stress and strain of a top London kitchen and the demands of the punters had got to him and he had popped under the pressure. He had bought the spider a few days previously, carried it around in his pocket, and just couldn't resist the temptation any longer – this was chef's revenge. How was he to know that it would land up on the table of the restaurant critic for *Harpers and Queen*?'
– *with thanks to TV personality and restaurant critic, Loyd Grossman.*

∞

The two girls who were engaged to the same man discovered each other's existence simultaneously. Rather than punishing each other, they decided to be thoroughly grown-up and controlled about it all and direct their revenge at him. The blonde telephone him: 'Darling,' she said, 'let's have a romantic lunch, just the two of us. See you at The Buck's Club at one.'

They made sure they arrived at the club after him. He was sitting at the table when they walked in together, dressed to the nines and both looking fantastic. Each picked up a different dish from the buffet, emptied it on his head, and calmly walked out again.

Photographic Evidence

'Never go to bed mad. Stay up and fight.'
Phyllis Diller

Photographic Evidence

In Italy, a hot-blooded lover was so distraught when his girlfriend said she was going back to her husband, that he had giant photographs printed of her in the nude. Then he plastered them over the entrance hall of her flat – and on the roof of her husband's car.

∞

A furious Frenchman took his revenge on his ex-girlfriend by advertising her in kinky contacts magazines. The adverts, some with photographs, claimed that a 21-year-old girl was 'seeking a virile man'. She received 946 replies, and it was over a year before the replies stopped arriving.

∞

A well-known photographer was having trouble getting a photograph of Bob Monkhouse which was needed for a television campaign for his new show. He had kept waiting for a week when, finally, he was invited to come and take the photograph just before one of the recordings. During the warm-up to the show, the photographer became the butt of Monkhouse's jokes about polaroids and haemorrhoids, and he did not take too kindly to it. To get his own back, he took all the photographs slightly out of the key light, which accentuated all the shadows and gave Mr Monkhouse double chins and a large nose that he did not deserve. To the photographer's delight, the photographs were duly displayed as part of the television campaign.

∞

Julia overheard her husband ordering flowers for his girl-friend. She immediately took polaroid photographs of his grubby underwear and their children and had them delivered with the husband's bouquet. He returned home that night with a black eye. They are now divorced.

∞

Tricia Morris took satisfying revenge on her cheating boyfriend, hockey player Graham Cook.

'I was humiliated and when we had a passionate weekend together an idea came into my head. I took a picture of him naked with his bottom in the air while he was getting dressed.' She then had a T-shirt printed with a giant photograph of his bare bum and wore it to his next match.

Cook was forced to flee ignominiously from the pitch as his fellow players collapsed with laughter when they saw their team-mate's blown-up botty and the caption 'Captain Cook's Tour Tart' emblazoned across Tricia's back.

∞

Pierette Le Pen, former wife of the French National Front party leader, carried out a most sophisticated sexual revenge. When she left her husband, the furious Jean-Marie refused to give her any money whatsoever and suggested that she might find a cleaning job to earn herself some extra francs. She took his advice and arranged a photographic shoot with *Playboy* magazine in which she cleaned, polished and swept wearing little more than a duster.

Travellers' Tales

— ∞ —

'Never complain, never explain – get even!'
Robert Kennedy

Travellers' Tales

The King of Morocco's brother, the late Prince Moulay Abdullah, took a chalet in Gstaad and it is alleged an unpopular member of the party needed quieting down. One evening he had too much to drink so the rest of the party took their revenge by putting one of his legs in plaster while he was unconscious.

In the morning he woke up, horrified to discover his leg immobilised from thigh to toe. The rest of the party made up a story about how he had had a terrible and dramatic fall and for the next week he complained how painful his leg was and how much he was suffering. Finally, when they could bear his martyrdom no more, they attacked his leg with a hammer to smash the plaster and he was hideously embarrassed when he discovered it was all a hoax.

∞

Some years ago Hugh and Judy Corbett were the happy owners of the sixteenth-century Dormy House Hotel set among trees on the Hereford/Worcester borders. Only once did they find guests so aggravating that they had to do something about it.

The particular guests were a couple of keen young Americans who stayed for five days, and drove Hugh mad, constantly asking what to do, where to go and then, on their return each day, giving him a full debrief each night about it all. Enough, Hugh thought.

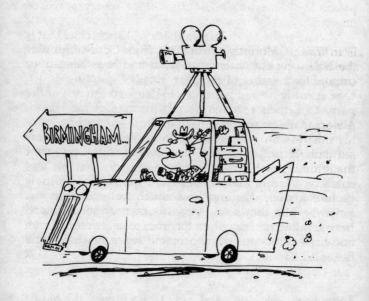

Their final morning they were to set off to Devon and wondered what they could do en route. 'Birmingham!' he announced proudly. 'The Venice of the north, with its beautiful waterways and parks, architecture not unlike Florence. I'll make you a picnic. Try to find your way to the Bull Ring to eat it. Marvellous place!' Complete with picnic the Americans set off with a merry wave of gratitude.

Anyone who knows Birmingham will appreciate that it is in quite the opposite direction from Devon and that the Bull Ring is a horrendously busy three-lane inner circular road surrounding office blocks.

∞

A woman discovered that her husband was going to take his mistress on a dirty weekend in Venice, which was particularly galling as that was where they had spent their honeymoon. He told her, however, that he was going on a business conference in Yorkshire.

His day of departure came and she had enormous fun following him round the house as he became more and more frantic in his search for his passport. He couldn't tell his wife what he was looking for and she was being overly helpful, secure in the knowledge that he would never look in the box of Tampax where she had hidden it.

∞

An Englishman was travelling through France some years ago. He knew he would be in Reims that night but would arrive late, so he telephoned a hotel to make the appropriate arrangements. He would like, he insisted, a room with a bathroom en suite. When he arrived at the hotel at around midnight, he was shown to his room and – no bathroom. He asked for a different room but no room with bathroom was available. Not having a choice he reluctantly moved in.

183

In the wee hours of the morning he felt the call of nature. The little handbasin would suit one purpose but there were other pressing matters. Spying a plant, he checked out the pot. Sure enough, it had not been watered for some time and the whole plant, earth and all, came out quite easily when lifted. He squatted over the pot and relieved himself, after which he squished the plant back in.

A couple of weeks later, when he was back in England, he received a letter from the hotel which went: *'Dear Sir, Since your stay with us in May we have been unable to rent out the room because of the smell. We know what it is, we would just be grateful if you could tell us where it is.'*

∞

A group of bright young things in Lausanne took a chalet in the Alps for the whole winter for holidays and weekends. A young lady who was a regular member of the houseparty started to get on everyone's nerves: she was always complaining, being the party pooper and generally making herself unpopular. They decided one night that enough was enough – action was needed. They took her lovely Alpha Romeo and, with a lot of spadework, buried it under a man-made snowdrift. She only found it in the Spring when the snows melted.

∞

Everybody on the holiday loathed the muscle-bound oaf (MBO) who strutted around the pool each day, flexing his pectorals and preening himself. He would lean against a surf-board or stand legs-apart-hands-on-hips like some ghastly parody of *Baywatch*, always in a prominent position so that the maximum number of people could admire him.

184

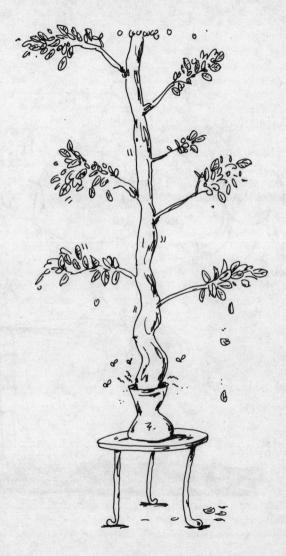

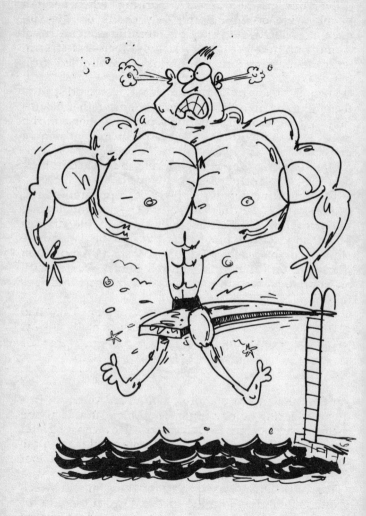

Everyone groaned as each morning, when enough people were occupying the easy chairs on the sun deck, the MBO would start his morning exercise ritual – one hundred press-ups, sit-ups, lean-and-stretch, with the morning sun glinting off his well-oiled, firm body.

Then, the body-building completed, he would strut to the end of the high diving-board, bounce rather beautifully and perform an irritatingly perfect somersault flip into the water with minimum splash and maximum grace.

Tired of having the metaphorical sand kicked in their eyes the other lads plotted his downfall.

The following morning the MBO appeared again, bronzed and beautiful. The routine began: the flexing, the pumping. Glistening, he walked to the diving-board and started his bounce. When he landed he slipped dramatically and undecorously, landed on the board on his bottom and fell into the water with an enormous and undignified splash, arms and legs flailing.

In unison the lads roared with laughter. They had coated the board with sun oil and the slick had made his performance anything but.

∞

An Englishman was standing behind an American in a queue checking in for a flight. The American was giving the poor check-in girl the full works – 'How can it be late? I need to be in Denver today, not tomorrow! Do you call this service? Whaddaya mean you won't upgrade me? Call yourself an airline?'

The Englishman was dazzled by her calm and sweet, sweet smile throughout the tirade. When it came to his turn, he asked her how she had remained so relaxed throughout his heated monologue. 'Don't worry,' she replied, 'I decided very early on that his luggage was going to Stuttgart.'

∞

A man was to spend a weekend abroad with someone he did not like and he was taking with him a visitor. To liven things up he told the visitor that his host was very deaf. He also told the host that his guest was deaf.

They spent the weekend shouting at each other.

Acting Up

— ∞ —

'No one delights more in vengeance than a woman.'

Juvenal, A.D. c.60–c.130

Acting Up

Derek Nimmo tours the Middle and Far East extensively. He is renowned in the business as a perfectionist and one night, during a performance in Hong Kong, things were not up to his exacting standards. He felt that the stage manager was not doing her job properly: various tea cups were out of place, a prop was missing and a doorbell came in late. Every time Mr Nimmo left the stage he would rage at the stage manager, who felt he was being unreasonable – had he never heard of mistakes?

The end of the performance arrived and, to tumultuous applause, he prepared to take a bow. As he started walking on to the stage the stage manager (who just happened to be his wife) brought the curtain down; right on top of him.

∞

Locked out in Anger. Playwright John Osborne could bear a grudge like no one else – and even managed to take revenge from beyond the grave. Those attending his memorial service in St Giles-in-the-Fields church in London, who included Lord Snowdon, Edward Fox, Sir Robin Day and Sir Dirk Bogarde, were surprised to see a notice outside which read: *'Memorial Service for John Osborne. The undermentioned will NOT be admitted. Their names are hereby posted on the gate: Fu Manchu, Nicholas de Jongh, Albert Finney, The Bard of Hay on Wye.'* Anyone familiar with the playwright's spite will know that Fu

Manchu is producer/director Sir Peter Hall and The Bard is playwright Arnold Wesker. Osborne, best known for his 1956 drama *Look Back in Anger*, was displeased by comments made by drama critic de Jongh and speculation was rife about the transgressions committed by the others singled out for non-admittance. To ensure that his wishes were carried out his wife, too, carried a copy of his request.

∞

When John Gilbert, a star among stars and Greta Garbo's most famous partner, died of heart failure at his Beverly Hill mansion, he was only thirty-eight years old.

After the funeral in 1936 plenty of cynics sneered that his career had died long before him – rakishly handsome 'Jack' Gilbert, once Hollywood's highest-paid leading man, was a victim of the talkies. The most notorious victim, really, for when movie audiences packed into *His Glorious Night* in 1929 and heard the romantic idol announce: 'I love you,' his squeaky tones reduced them to shocked laughter. Film buffs repeat the story to this day. But the odds are that they have bought a myth. It is far more likely that Gilbert was destroyed in the sort of vendetta possible only when moguls walked the earth and studios reigned supreme, because Gilbert, rash and outspoken as any hero he played in a hundred or so films, had made a bitter enemy of Louis B Mayer, boss of MGM.

Mayer was a monster, of course, but even monsters have soft spots. With Mayer it was Motherhood – a man owed everything to his mother, the mogul insisted, and men failing to respect and adore their mothers were beyond the pale. Gilbert scorned and detested Mayer, was well aware of his prejudices and set out to strike his raw nerve.

The chance came in the twenties, when Louis B Mayer

was holding forth to his minions. He would have no truck with screen versions of *Anna Christie* or *Camille*, he spluttered, because the central characters were immoral women.

'What's wrong with that?' John Gilbert inquired innocently. 'My own mother was a whore.' According to one onlooker's version, Mayer had to be physically restrained from hitting the actor. Certainly he loathed the man ever afterwards, and there are persuasive clues that the head of MGM set out to sabotage one of his top box-office draws. Crazy? Not by Hollywood standards.

The fact is that MGM sound technician Douglas Shearer testified: 'We never turned up the bass when Gilbert spoke – all you heard was the treble.' And Shearer wasn't just any old sound man; his sister was the actress Norma Shearer, who also happened to be Mrs Irving Thalberg, wife of the studio's brilliant young production chief. Thanks to Hollywood nepotism, Douglas was close to the kingdom's heart. Could Louis B Mayer have been vengeful and irresponsible enough to spike his own firm's guns and pollute its product by ordering that a $250,000-per-picture performer be made to sound ridiculous? In a word – easily! For the story of Jack Gilbert's squeaky 'I love you' has Byzantine complications.

Mayer ran MGM in Hollywood but the ultimate shots were called by Nick Schenck, New York-based president of the parent company, Loew's Inc. Resenting Schenck's power, Mayer constantly denigrated him and Mayer was furious when, just as he determined to break Jack Gilbert, axe him and make him unemployable, Nick Schenck went behind his back and signed the mother-mocking star to a four-picture contract worth $1m. Ensuring that Gilbert's first talkie was a fiasco would have killed two of Mayer's birds with one stone – menaced his victim's career *and* made Schenck seem foolish for betting a million bucks on the wrong horse.

Facts clash with received wisdom that John Gilbert was ruined by the talkies. After all he appeared in nine more movies after his sound debut, so his voice can't have been all that unacceptable. Vintage sound-tracks and recordings of Thirties radio interviews suggest that Gilbert had a light, not particularly high voice, no better nor worse than scores of actors who made a smooth transfer from silent films. What emerges over the years, as Mayer's death loosened studio tongues, is that tragic Gilbert wasn't killed by the talkies but his heavy drinking – and the revenge of Louis B Mayer.
– *an insight into Hollywood by kind courtesy of film writer, Shaun Usher.*

∞

'I'm ashamed of this story. I like actors very much and seldom find bitching on the stage, but on one occasion I was sorely tried.

'One of the male stars in the play behaved very badly, and with such arrogance that life became miserable for us all. As far as I was concerned my trouble was that, for some reason, he refused to give me my entrance cue. I asked him very nicely if he would do so, and he looked at me coldly and said "No." I asked why, and he replied, "It doesn't interest me," and when I said, "But how do I know when to come on?" he answered, "Please yourself." So I did.

'It was a breakfast scene, and he had made up a very funny piece of business where he choked over his coffee cup. I decided to teach him a lesson. I arrived on stage earlier than he expected, swooped happily towards him crooning "Good morning, good morning", slapped him hard on his bald head with a rolled up newspaper and, as he was about to pick up the cup, removed it and left the stage, briskly and with no further dialogue. The actor who should have followed me on was unprepared so the

rogue star was left entirely alone, and totally speechless with rage. He never behaved badly to me again.'
– *with thanks to Dulcie Gray, actress and author.*

∞

'It was my first job as an Assistant Stage Manager and I was, unfortunately, working with a monstrous actress. She did everything to make my life hell. Five minutes before going on stage she would pull her pearls off from round her neck so that they scattered all over the floor and demand that the Assistant Stage Manager pick them up immediately and string them together. Her bad behaviour was endless and caused much grief. The time had arrived when I had had enough.

'Her exit at the end of the play was a dramatic one, she would grab her bag from the sofa and sweep off the stage to tumultuous applause. However, on this particular night, a stage weight had been placed in her bag. As she took her bag the weight was so immense that it forced her to collapse, face first, on to the sofa.'
– *with thanks to Roger Redfarn, theatrical director.*

∞

'There was an amusing incident in Los Angeles which happened to Jack when he was out there "pitching" ideas, i.e., selling himself to the youngest, most fresh-faced twelve-year-old moguls he could find. After one exhausting day beating what was left of his brains out to blank faces, he arrived in the office of another tiny tyrant at around 6.30 in the evening. The secretary had already left so he waited patiently in the lobby.

'The mogul's door was slightly open and he heard through the aperture a voice on the phone saying "No, I can't get away for another hour, honey. I've got to see some shmock from England." More twittery goodbye noises followed, at the end of which Jack strode down the

corridor, opened the door of the office, poked his head in with a big grin on his face and said "Hello, I'm the shmock from England. Where are you a shmock from?"

'The big cheese had the grace to apologise and during the meeting that followed further endeared himself to Mr Rosenthal by saying that his company, "Movie of the Week", dealt in three areas only: heart, stomach and groin. Seeing Jack's expression, he elaborated: "Heart is romance, stomach is horror and groin is sexploitation." Jack nodded gravely, stood up and said, "I'm sorry, this is not for me. I'm afraid I only do 'elbow'." The mogul was impressed; he wanted to know more but Jack just smiled and left enigmatically.

'The following day at 9 o'clock in the morning, the guy with the world at his feet and his feet six inches off the floor, phoned Jack's agent and said, "Get me the guy who writes elbow, I gotta have him. Elbow's exactly what we are looking for." By this time, Mr Rosenthal was on a plane halfway across the Atlantic, rubbing elbows with real people . . .'

– with thanks to actress and writer Maureen Lipman who tells us this story about her husband, the writer Jack Rosenthal.

∞

'I was asked to provide the voice of a donkey for a commercial extolling the virtues of a well-known West Country resort. I shall not reveal the place or the firm concerned for fear of embarrassment. The recording was carried out all very efficiently and the character of the cheery little donkey seemed to come through well enough to keep the client happy. It was a tortuous day in which I drew on all my classical training at Rose Bruford and with Jaques Lecoq in Paris. If only Stanislavski could have seen the preparation for this role.

'Having completed the job the invoice was sent and it was just a question of waiting for the cheque.

WRONG . . . three weeks turned to four, from a month to two, three . . . six months passed and no cheque. I sent the "kind" letter along, "I wonder if you have forgotten?", "I wonder if you have mislaid the invoice?", all that sort of polite remindery! After seven months I had had enough. It wasn't as if it was thousands of pounds. It was peanuts considering how my voice had suffered as that ruddy donkey.

'I decided on a different tack: confront them and get to see "Mr Big", the man with the money. I went into the office which was situated in Bristol. Nice area. Nice carpet, I recall. Nobody in the office except the receptionist-cum-secretary-cum-tea and coffee makeress. "Excuse me," I said, "I believe I am owed some money, can I have it please?" I showed all the relevant documents. The phone calls began, furtive looks at me and I smile. "Yes, Mr Harris, it's in hand. You should get it soon." "I want it now," I said. "It's already seven months late." "You'll just have to be patient," the woman said. That did it. I crossed quietly to the desk, unplugged the best-looking typewriter and made for the door. "Excuse meeeeeeeee . . ." she said, "what do you think you are doing?" "I'll take this in place of the money if that is all right with you," I said.

'The door was already beginning to close. "Just a minute," she said . . . more phone calls and I began to wilt under the weight of the IBM, or whatever it was. Click, the phone goes down. "All right, Mr Harris, the cheque is in the post." Yarooooooo!!! Success at last!

'I should point out that such behaviour is out of character for me. Totally out of character. I suffered for weeks imagining the moment I pulled out the plug – my clammy hands slip, the prickly heat begins and the firm arm of the law descends. Ohhh cripes!!! However, it was all worthwhile as I got my hard-earned lolly.'
– *with thanks to Chris Harris, theatre director.*

Quick Tricks and
Devilish Deeds

Quick Tricks and Devilish Deeds

There was a man who achieved far better results than he could have hoped for by tipping out the shampoo from the bottle in her shower and substituting it with golden syrup.

∞

1471 has made anonymous telephone calls traceable, but canny callers know that if they dial 141 before making the call, it renders the call untraceable.

∞

Ordinary rosehips contain a marvellous home-made itching powder. The minute, hairy fibres, when dried, pierce the skin and cause considerable irritation. There is no end to the creative ideas for their use.

∞

Make a video recording of your loo (with no-one in it). Next time there is a party, wait until someone goes to the lavatory. While he (or she) is there, put on your video. When he comes back he'll think you've all been watching him.

∞

Post something appropriate to your adversary. We know of one woman who posted her erstwhile lover an anchovy.

∞

Senna powder can have a dramatic effect, particularly if stewed. The man into whose bran flakes it was put knew of the fabled effect of bran but was surprised by its vehemence.

∞

Milk is the stuff of vengeance and full fat ripens best – especially when it is tipped on to a carpet or, better still, the floor of the car.

∞

If you know somebody you can't stand who has a pager number, find somebody else who they can't stand and page one to call the other, many times.

∞

Put confetti in the air vent of their car.

∞

Insert a siren into the exhaust pipe of their car.

∞

Arrange for your victim's neighbour to receive a pornographic magazine in their mail with the victim's name but the wrong house number on the label.

∞

There are a number of surprises you can put in the water tank – cochineal, washing-up liquid, blackcurrant juice – the possibilities are endless.

∞

Why not put cows in your ex-lover's basement? Cows will go down stairs but they will not go up!

∞

Fix fake number plates on the back of their car which look real and say things like: B J KING, DICKLESS or I AM GAY. It can take weeks before they notice.

∞

Have some fun re-recording your ex-partner's outgoing answerphone message. The possibilities are endless.

∞

Scatter a few pounds of raw mince over his/her lawn. It attracts all kinds of wild and domestic animals, not to mention maggots.

∞

A man in New York poured sugar behind the plaster on the walls. They had to tear the walls out to get rid of the resulting cockroach problem.

∞

Collect lots of call girls' phone numbers (you can always find plenty of their call cards in telephone boxes) and leave these numbers on your victim's pager.

∞

One little boy who had been persistently bullied placed a sardine at the bottom of the bully's locker.

∞

Put a fish in the ventilation shaft.

∞

Put a big glob of grease under his car door handle.

∞

If your victim has a fax number get five or six pieces of black paper, dial their number and let the fax begin. Don't

I'M SORRY I CAN'T COME TO THE 'PHONE JUST AT THE MOMENT — I'M HAVING SEX WITH A SMALL GOAT — BUT IF YOU'D LIKE TO LEAVE YOUR NAME AND NUMBER I'LL GET BACK TO YOU AS SOON AS I CAN ....

forget to erase your number from the machine. This will cost the recipient a lot of money, especially if they use the very costly thermal fax paper – and have you priced toner cartridges lately? Of course it will be expensive on your phone bill unless you use someone else's fax machine.

∞

For those connected to the Internet: mail bomb him with gibberish text files, 30k or so long. Send several hundred copies to him in order to fill his mail box.

∞

Put his name and phone number on the Internet, asking lots and lots of people to call him. Internet users are an active bunch and keen to please.

∞

Call the home shopping network and order hundreds of pounds' worth of things for her. Make sure you use *her* phone number!

∞

Call every kind of business that has an answering machine and leave a message for each in the mark's name expressing a desire to spend lots of money with the firm – pick the really sleazy ones.

∞

Tell her she looks absolutely wonderful in that simply frightful dress she is dithering about buying.

∞

Unscrew the shower head and put in a little powdered or crystallised pigment or colourant.

∞

Tell the Inland Revenue about the cash job your target did for you.

∞

Stick a matchstick in her keyhole and break off the end.

∞

Tell him you're pregnant.

∞

Tell him you're pregnant and it's not his.

∞

Always do your own dirty work – if you have assistants they can turn on you.

∞

When staying in a hotel with someone you dislike, order a fabulous breakfast consisting of everything on the entire menu, to be delivered to their room . . . at 5.00a.m.!

∞

Skiers who are fed up with queue-bargers and other irritants might employ this method of revenge. If the gondola lift has one of those compartments where the skis and poles are carried *outside* the lift it is a simple matter to wait until the lift is about to depart . . . and quietly remove the skis. It causes untold irritation to the victim that they have to go all the way up in the lift – and then down again to collect their skis.
– with thanks to the younger members of the Palmer-Tomkinson family who assure us they have never done it themselves!

∞

Bobbit!

HAVE YOU HEARD
OF A BETTER
REVENGE STORY?

PLEASE TELL US!

PLEASE WRITE TO US AT:
PO BOX 3054,
LONDON SW6 2HG

A Greater Love
Charles & Camilla

Christopher Wilson

– THE ENDURING LOVE AFFAIR THAT ROCKED THE ROYAL FAMILY

In July 1994, Prince Charles finally admitted in a television interview with Jonathan Dimbleby that he had committed adultery with Camilla Parker Bowles. His admission shocked the nation; now, in *A Greater Love*, Christopher Wilson charts the full story of the love affair between Charles and Camilla from its early days over twenty years ago.

How could an apparently plain and unintelligent woman have captivated Prince Charles so completely for so long? How did the affair survive both Camilla's marriage to Andrew Parker Bowles, and Charles' marriage to Diana? Was it responsible for the break-up of Charles and Diana's marriage?

This sensationally frank book reveals for the first time the true character of Camilla Parker Bowles, and describes in detail the complex nature of Charles and Camilla's ill-starred romance – a romance which has gravely damaged the Royal Family.

NON-FICTION / BIOGRAPHY 0 7472 4676 9

More Self Help from Headline

Across a Crowded Room

HOW TO FIND AND KEEP THE LOVE OF YOUR LIFE

Sue Plumtree

Love is in the air . . .

Meeting and keeping friends and lovers can be a minefield of
misunderstandings and uncertainty. Sue Plumtree's unique
guide throws light on each stage of the way. Discover how to
deal with fear of rejection, how to develop your self-esteem, the
art of being happy, what makes and breaks relationships and
how to recognise the right partner for you.

You can make things happen for yourself. You just have to start
as you mean to go on. Meeting people is fun. You can develop a
conversation. You can ask people out and enjoy yourself. When
you find someone you like, this book helps you to grow and
nurture a fragile young relationship into something strong and
rewarding.

Whether you would like to be in a relationship or to improve the
one you are already in, Sue Plumtree's down-to-earth humorous
approach makes everything possible.

'The woman is a delight.' Lyndsay Russell, *Independent*

'All extremely good sense and very timely in view of the
considerable confusion and hurt that can follow, these days,
when a man and a woman attempt to establish a loving
relationship.' Tom Crabtree, *Cosmopolitan*

NON-FICTION / SELF HELP 0 7472 4789 7

More Sparkling Humour from Headline

DATES FROM HELL

Maryon Tysoe

Whatever you have been through, it can't be as bad as the true stories of the worst-ever, funniest-ever

DATES FROM HELL

Even if you have been discarded like an old shoe, squashed flat as a hedgehog on the road or humiliated to what seems the point of no return, it is always the greatest comfort to know that other people have suffered dating disasters even more excruciating than yours. While they won't mend a broken heart, these gripping accounts might just stop you from retiring into monastic seclusion! As every survivor of the dating game will tell you, your sense of humour is the strongest defence you have. So, even if you can't see the funny side of your own fiasco yet, *Dates From Hell* will remind you of one vital fact: the hell you're living through today will make for a great story tomorrow!

NON-FICTION / HUMOUR 0 7472 4572 X

A selection of non-fiction from Headline